A MONUMENT TO DYNASTY AND DEATH

WITNESS TO ANCIENT HISTORY

Gregory S. Aldrete, *Series Editor*

A MONUMENT TO DYNASTY AND DEATH

The Story of
Rome's Colosseum
and the Emperors
Who Built It

Nathan T. Elkins

Johns Hopkins University Press
Baltimore

© 2019 Johns Hopkins University Press
All rights reserved. Published 2019
Printed in the United States of America on acid-free paper

2   4   6   8   9   7   5   3   1

Johns Hopkins University Press
2715 North Charles Street
Baltimore, Maryland 21218-4363
www.press.jhu.edu

Library of Congress Cataloging-in-Publication Data

Names: Elkins, Nathan T.
Title: A monument to dynasty and death : the story of Rome's Colosseum
and the emperors who built it / Nathan T. Elkins.
Description: Baltimore, MD : Johns Hopkins University Press, [2019] |
Series: Witness to ancient history | Includes bibliographical references
and index.
Identifiers: LCCN 2018057301 | ISBN 9781421432540 (hardcover :
alk. paper) | ISBN 9781421432557 (pbk. : alk. paper) | ISBN 9781421432564
(electronic) | ISBN 1421432544 (hardcover : alk. paper) | ISBN 1421432552
(pbk. : alk. paper) | ISBN 1421432560 (electronic)
Subjects: LCSH: Colosseum (Rome, Italy)—History. | Colosseum (Rome,
Italy)—Design and construction. | Amphitheaters—Italy—Rome. |
Games—Rome—History. | Emperors—Rome—History. | Rome
(Italy)—Buildings, structures, etc. | Rome (Italy)—Antiquities.
Classification: LCC DG68.1 .E44 2019 | DDC 937/.63—dc23
LC record available at https://lccn.loc.gov/2018057301

A catalog record for this book is available from the British Library.

Special discounts are available for bulk purchases of this book.
For more information, please contact Special Sales at 410-516-6936
or specialsales@press.jhu.edu.

Johns Hopkins University Press uses environmentally friendly book
materials, including recycled text paper that is composed of at least
30 percent post-consumer waste, whenever possible.

To Steven L. Tuck, one of the best professors an undergraduate could have, with whom I first laid eyes on the Colosseum during his "Rome of the Caesars" study abroad program at the end of my freshman year

CONTENTS

A MONUMENT TO DYNASTY AND DEATH

PROLOGUE

Opening Day at the Colosseum

EARLY ONE MORNING in 80 CE, the Colosseum roared to life with the deafening cheers of tens of thousands of spectators as the emperor, Titus, mounted his tribunal to inaugurate the new amphitheater with 100 days of bloody spectacles in the city of Rome. These games were much anticipated, for the new amphitheater had been under construction for a decade. The crowd grew silent as a procession carrying images and attributes of the gods and deified emperors entered the arena, followed by the wild beasts and gladiators who would perform in the games that day. Musical accompaniment enhanced the liveliness of the procession and built anticipation for the long day of entertainment. After the procession, the morning hours were filled with violent animal spectacles. Bedecked with scenery, the arena floor resembled a wild habitat, perhaps a jungle, in order to make the hunts more interesting and unpredictable. Trained hunters stalked and killed exotic beasts imported from the corners of the Roman Empire, including tigers, lions, leopards, and bears, although more common and less threatening animals, such as deer, were also hunted in the arena. Hunters typically killed their prey, but the crowd loved to cheer for the animals and reveled in the maiming and mauling of beast fighters. The Romans pitted animals against one another as well. Common predator and prey animals, such as dogs and deer or dogs and hares, were often set loose to confront one another and to entertain the crowds. Exotic animals were also made to combat each other. Martial, the poet, and an eyewitness to the earliest spectacles in the Colosseum, describes a rhinoceros tossing a bull into the air as if it were a toy; he also reports an encounter in which an elephant thrashed a bull.[1]

At the lunch hour, respectable citizens may have taken a break to dine outside the amphitheater, but tens of thousands remained to watch the execution of condemned criminals, who were put to death in violent, staged mythological enactments. Martial provides a flavor of such executions in his vivid description of one criminal who was bound to a cross or pole on the arena floor and, while alive and helplessly exposed, was shredded by a bear imported from Caledonia (modern Scotland) until his limbs dripped with blood and gore and life eventually flowed from his tired and tortured body.[2] We can only imagine the sights and sounds that filled the amphitheater at that hour: the ominous grunts and growls of the advancing bear, probably enraged by taunts and ravaged by starvation to increase its ferocity; the screams of the crucified criminal, lacerated and devoured by the beast; and the clamor of the crowd, at one moment cheering in celebration of the violence and just punishment and, at the next, groaning at the gruesome sight. All the while spectators dined on snacks, sold at concessions nearby or within the Colosseum itself, as they watched the lives of combatants, both human and animal, meet their end.

The afternoon and early evening hosted the main event: gladiatorial combats. Spectators may have leapt to their feet and shouted with joy as the first two swords met that day. There was power in the crowd's tenor, for at the end of a gladiatorial match the emperor made a life-or-death decision regarding the fate of the defeated gladiator; the emperor measured the sentiments of the spectators to determine whether the gladiator fought well and should live or whether the victor should dispatch him. At the end of the day, scores of animals and people lay dead. The sands of the arena were mucked with sweat and blood, and the scent of death and iron lingered in the air, masked somewhat by the smell of saffron with which the crowd had been sprayed. It was just day one—the crowd would return for another 99 days to complete this set of inaugural games that would claim the lives of thousands of animals and an untold number of gladiators and condemned criminals.

As grand and bloody as the 100 days of games were, the primary venue for these unprecedented spectacles was no less spectacular. This book not only tells the story of the construction of the Colosseum under Vespasian, its dedication under Titus, and Domitian's enhancements to the building but also explores the political and ideological significance of the Colosseum for the emperors of this family, the Flavian dynasty. The building itself was a marvel, slowly rising to dominate the skyline of Rome in the valley to the southeast of the Forum Romanum as the people anticipated the day they could enter and enjoy the great amphitheater's comforts and relish its spectacles.

The Flavian Amphitheater, probably called simply the *amphitheatrum* by the Romans, became known as the Colosseum in the Middle Ages and still popularly bears that name. It was the largest and grandest of all amphitheaters in the Roman Empire, with some strikingly modern amenities that foreshadowed today's sports stadiums. The amphitheater rises in height to 48.5 meters (159 feet), approximately the height of a 15-story building today, and its footprint occupies an area of about 24,000 square meters (nearly 260,000 square feet, or approximately six acres). The Colosseum also has elaborate substructures that would have allowed an army of slaves and servicemen to raise gladiators, animals, stage props, and scenery efficiently and dramatically to the arena floor above. A great awning, deployed from wooden masts and over an elaborate system of rigging at the top of the amphitheater with an opening over the arena floor, shaded spectators from the hot Italian sun in a way that is not dissimilar from modern stadiums with retractable roofs. Eighty entrances pierce the amphitheater's façade, and all were marked with Roman numerals, except for the four special entrances on the long and short axes. A spectator's ticket would have corresponded with a specific entrance that would have connected him or her efficiently with a system of barriers and staircases that led to the appropriate seating section. According to modern estimates, the Colosseum could seat 50,000 to 55,000 spectators, although an ancient source, the Chronographer of 354 CE, states that it could accommodate 87,000. One could enjoy snacks at a day of games and use water fountains and flushing toilets, as in modern sports stadiums. A spectator might also scrawl graffiti on his seat relating to the games he was witnessing or draw something vulgar in the corridor on his return from the toilet, as do some sports fans at stadiums today.

After Vespasian had ordered its construction, nearly a decade before its inauguration, the growing hulk of stone and concrete, which would become the largest and most advanced building for the gladiatorial combats and arena spectacles in the totality of the Roman Empire, stoked the anticipation of Rome's population as it witnessed the structure take shape. The urban populace looked forward to the day of the Colosseum's inauguration, as Rome had lacked the proper venue for amphitheater games for many years. The city had possessed the small, stone Amphitheater of Statilius Taurus, dedicated in 30 BCE, and Nero had built a wooden amphitheater for the urban masses in 57 CE. The Great Fire of 64 CE had, however, destroyed those amphitheaters. Rome was in need of a new, grand amphitheater. The Flavian emperors filled that need and, in doing so, promoted their own political position.

The Colosseum was far more than a lavish entertainment building to host gory spectacles for the amusement of the Roman people; it was an ideologically charged monument to the aspirations and achievements of the new dynasty. Vespasian, the founder of the Flavian dynasty, began construction on the Colosseum on the site of what was the great lake in the *atrium* of Nero's Golden House (Domus Aurea), which Nero had built on land appropriated after the Great Fire of 64 CE and which had occupied a significant portion of the city. The dismantling of Nero's palace contrasted the new regime with the ill-remembered Nero, whose maladministration forced the provinces into rebellion, resulting in the emperor's suicide, the end of the Julio-Claudian dynasty, and a bloody civil war.

The Colosseum should be viewed not as a monument built in isolation but as part of a broader complex of Flavian buildings in the area of what was Nero's Domus Aurea. Understanding the relationship of these monuments together informs the political context and ideological agenda. Near the Colosseum were gladiator schools, the Meta Sudans fountain, the Baths of Titus, and the Temple of the Deified Claudius. The repurposing of the area of the Domus Aurea for popular use painted Nero as a selfish tyrant, while presenting the Flavians as restorers of Rome. As Nero's memory was attacked by the destruction and transformation of the Domus Aurea, the construction of the Colosseum and some of the monuments around it ideologically linked the new dynasty with deified members of the former dynasty. The dedication of a great amphitheater in the heart of the city of Rome was presented as the fulfillment of a grand ambition of Augustus, connecting the new dynasty with the revered and deified founder of the empire.[3] The realization of the Meta Sudans fountain next to the Colosseum also reinforced an ideological connection with the Deified Augustus, for he had built a fountain here. Vespasian's dutiful completion of the Temple of the Deified Claudius on the Caelian Hill, just south of the Colosseum, also aligned the new dynasty with the last "good" emperor of the Julio-Claudian dynasty. The Colosseum was also a monument to Flavian victory, as Vespasian and Titus quelled the Jewish Revolt and celebrated a triumph in Rome. Representations of the Colosseum show an entrance elaborated in the form of a triumphal arch surmounted by a chariot driven by four horses (a *quadriga*), symbolizing Flavian victory. Additionally, an inscription from the Colosseum states explicitly that the Flavians financed its construction with the spoils of war. Thus, more than a monumental venue for deadly games, for the Flavians the Colosseum was a complex monument to Flavian rule and hegemony—a monument to their dynasty.

-I-

The Rise of a New Dynasty

THE COLOSSEUM, THE BEST-KNOWN ancient monument in Europe, is immediately recognizable and embedded in modern culture. It is the main setting for the Hollywood film *Gladiator* (2000), with Russell Crowe playing the lead character (Maximus), and numerous other "sword-and-sandal" films set in ancient Rome; it appears also in countless other movies of different genres, set in different periods. The Colosseum is a popular emblem of Rome and Italy. Invariably, images of the Colosseum are everywhere one looks when visiting the modern city; in souvenir shops, it is ubiquitous, appearing on post-cards, books, calendars, t-shirts, handbags, pillows, prints, and other media. To the beat of techno music, spray-paint artists using stencils frantically crank out fantastical images of the famous amphitheater on the busy streets nearby and hawk them to tourists. The five-cent Euro coins for Italy even feature the Colosseum. Despite the Colosseum's iconic status and familiarity in modern popular culture, few people outside of academic circles are conversant with the political events and rich history that led to the construction and dedication of the greatest amphitheater that the Romans ever built. To understand the circumstances that led to the construction of the Colosseum, one must go back to the reign of Nero (54–68 CE) and specifically to the events of 64 CE and their aftermath.

Nero's Downfall and the End of the Julio-Claudian Dynasty

Everyone has heard the fanciful line, "Nero fiddled while Rome burned." The popular expression refers to Nero's facility with the lyre, the tyrannical character attributed to him by Roman authors after his death, and the Great Fire of 64 CE, which devastated much of the city of Rome. The saying derives from Suetonius, the second-century CE biographer, who claims that Nero had set fire to the city and then watched from a tower in the Gardens of Maecenas while singing the "Sack of Ilium (Troy)" and strumming the lyre in his performance garb.[1] Of course, Suetonius's biographies often include gossip as source material, and this account is hardly believable. According to Tacitus, the second-century CE historian, the emperor was in Antium when the Great Fire began, and Nero's response was more positive. He says that Nero returned to the city and opened the Campus Martius (the Field of Mars) and his own gardens to house those displaced by the fire (figure 1.1); he also ordered food to be brought from Ostia, Rome's port city, to relieve the people, and he reduced the price of grain.[2] After the fire, Nero instituted several reforms and regulations to guard against such devastating conflagrations in the future. For instance, he began to enforce the limits that Augustus (27 BCE–14 CE), the first Roman emperor, had imposed on the heights of buildings, insisted on the use of more stone construction to retard the spread of fire, and also determined that streets should be wider so that it would be more difficult for fire to pass from building to building.[3] While it is improbable that Nero orchestrated the burning of the capital, he did indeed exploit the calamity by appropriating much of the land consumed by the fire to build a great palace called the Domus Aurea, or Golden House, a building complex to which we shall return at the end of this chapter.

Roman authors portray Nero as a selfish and cruel ruler. He became emperor at the age of 17 when his adopted father, the emperor Claudius (41–54 CE), died. In the Roman world, adoption had equal force to blood relation, which made Nero the heir apparent when Claudius married Nero's mother, Agrippina, and adopted him, her son from a previous marriage. This gave Nero precedence over Claudius's own son by birth, Britannicus. Roman writers say that Claudius died after he was fed poisonous mushrooms; Agrippina allegedly conceived of the plot, so that her son would ascend to the role of emperor.[4] Initially, Agrippina exerted much influence over Nero but clashed with his tutor, Seneca, and the commander of the Praetorian Guard (the emperor's personal bodyguard and a large military force stationed in Rome). She lost Nero's affections after interfering in his romantic affairs and began to offer support to the young Britan-

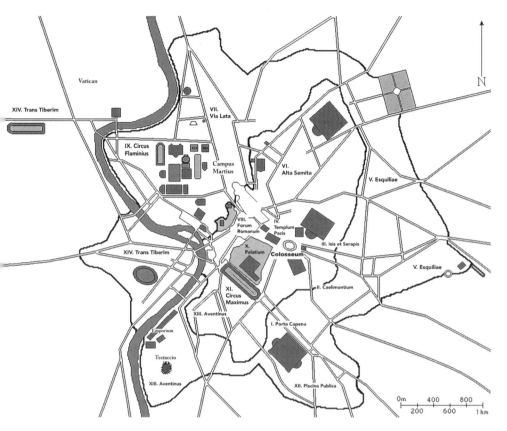

Figure 1.1. Plan of Rome showing the location of the Colosseum, after Nero's death, in relation to the topography of the city (Joris1919 from nl/Wikimedia Commons)

nicus as a potential rival to her son. Just a few months after Nero took office, Britannicus died by poisoning at Nero's command in February 55 CE, the day before his fourteenth birthday.[5] In 59 CE, Nero dispatched his mother. According to the ancient sources, he invited Agrippina to dine with him at Baiae, a city on the Bay of Naples; to travel there, she mounted a barge that had been rigged to collapse at sea so that she would be crushed by the wreckage and die in the ocean. Nevertheless, she survived the wreck, swam to shore, and returned to her villa. When Nero heard of this, he sent his guardsmen to kill her.[6] The emperor developed a bad relationship with the senatorial aristocracy, and many of his advisers and confidants fell out of favor, accused of various crimes and conspiracies. Nero's construction of a large palace in the center of the city, and its accessibility to all of Rome's citizenry, may have also fueled the discontent of Rome's upper classes.

Fed up with Nero's style of governance, the senator Gaius Calpurnius Piso marshaled a conspiracy in 65 CE that involved several senators, prominent equestrians (a property-based social class that ranked just under the senatorial class), and a joint commander of the Praetorian Guard.[7] The plot was uncovered, and Piso, the Praetorian commander, and many other conspirators were put to death or forced to commit suicide. Seneca, Lucan, and Petronius were among the Roman intellectual elites who died for their alleged involvement in the conspiracy. Without a doubt, the quelling of the conspiracy and the deaths of many noblemen exacerbated the uneasiness of the senators.

Nero's commitment to his personal diversions may have worsened his autocratic character. He was an avid Hellenophile, having devoted himself to the lyre, poetry, and music, and he had also instituted Greek-style athletic competitions in Rome, which found little popularity there compared with more traditional Roman forms of entertainment, such as chariot races and gladiatorial combats. In 66–67 CE, he toured Greece and participated in the Olympic Games. It was during this time, in 66 CE, that the Roman province of Judaea (modern Israel/Palestine) rebelled against Roman rule (figure 1.2). Titus Flavius Vespasianus (Vespasian, emperor 69–79 CE) had been in Nero's entourage during his tour of Greece, but the emperor had dismissed him because he had offended the emperor when he either walked out of one of his recitals or fell asleep at a performance. After his dismissal, Vespasian was hiding out in a small town in fear of Nero's wrath.[8] But in 67 CE, Vespasian's talents were in need, and Nero gave him a military command to quash the rebellion in Judaea. Vespasian was thus in a strategic position when Nero died, and the question of who would succeed him as emperor was settled by civil war.

The end finally came for Nero in 68 CE when another province rebelled. Gaius Julius Vindex, the governor of Gallia Lugdunensis (a province in what is now the northwestern coastal region and part of central France), took up arms against Nero and declared his support for Servius Sulpicius Galba, the governor of Hispania Terraconensis in northeastern Spain (the largest province in that territory). The Neronian loyalist Lucius Verginius Rufus, governor of Germania Superior (Upper Germany), soon defeated Vindex, but the rebellion could not be stopped, for Galba had taken up Vindex's call to arms against Nero. After defeating Vindex, Rufus's soldiers proclaimed him emperor, but the patriot refused. Support continued to build for Galba to the point that the commander of the Praetorian Guard abandoned Nero and offered Galba the support of this large armed force in the capital. Nero fled Rome and intended to travel to a loyal province where he could regroup and regain control over the

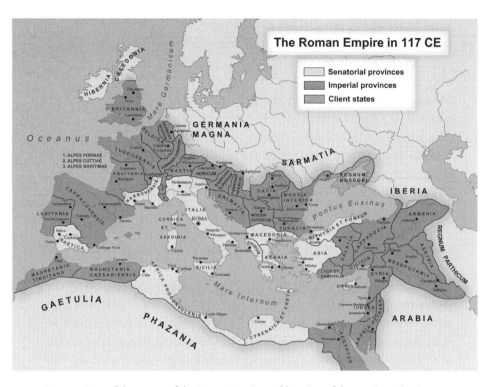

Figure 1.2. Map of the extent of the Roman Empire and location of the provinces in circa 117 CE (Andrei Nacu/Wikimedia Commons, with modifications by Lisa Fehsenfeld)

rebellious factions. But upon learning that the Senate also had abandoned him, declaring him a public enemy, Nero resolved to commit suicide. While preparing for death, he proclaimed, "What an artist dies in me!"[9] Unable to muster the will to plunge the sword into his own chest, he enlisted the help of his secretary to kill him. With Nero's death, and no designated heir to succeed him, the Julio-Claudian dynasty that had ruled the Roman Empire for nearly 100 years (27 BCE–68 CE) collapsed and the empire was embroiled in civil war.[10]

The Year of the Four Emperors: 69 CE

After Nero's suicide, Galba, who had previously allowed himself to be called only the legate of the Senate and Roman People while answering Vindex's charge to lead hostilities against Nero, took on imperial titles and was recognized as the emperor; he marched on Rome to secure his position in the capital.[11] Galba's reign was short lived. After becoming emperor on June 9, 68 CE, he was killed on January 15, 69 CE. Galba's lack of popularity contributed to his downfall. During his invasion of Italy he was harsh with towns that resisted him, and once in Rome he ordered the executions of senators. In addition, he repealed many of Nero's popular reforms, which garnered him no affection from the urban masses. When he took office, Galba replaced Lucius Verginius Rufus, the governor of Upper Germany who had defeated Vindex, with Aulus Vitellius. That turned out to be a fatal mistake, for at the New Year the legions under Vitellius's command refused to take the annual oath of loyalty to the emperor and instead proclaimed Vitellius to be their emperor. With Upper Germany and its legions in rebellion, the Roman Empire was plunged into another civil war just seven months after Nero had died.

In response to the rebellion, Galba hastily adopted Lucius Calpurnius Piso Licinianus as his heir, which greatly offended the senator Marcus Salvius Otho, who had expected to become Galba's heir apparent. Upset with this turn of events, Otho easily purchased the loyalty of the Praetorian Guard. The Praetorians already had no love for Galba, because he had refused to give them a special payment that they expected after he came to power. The Praetorians killed both Galba and Piso in the Forum Romanum and brought Galba's head to Otho. Resentful guardsmen jeered at and mocked Galba's severed head in the Praetorian camp.

Otho's reign was also brief. Taking office immediately after Galba's murder on January 15, 69 CE, he died just three months later on April 16. Vitellius's armies were marching on Rome and, despite Otho's attempts to negotiate a peace, their respective armies met at Bedriacum (near modern Cremona, Italy), where Otho's forces were defeated. Otho took his own life by stabbing himself in the chest.

The Senate immediately recognized Vitellius as Rome's emperor; his reign would last only eight months, for he was killed on December 21, 69 CE. The ancient sources suggest that Vitellius was not only self-indulgent but cruel, in part due to his paranoia about potential conspiracies and challengers. In July of 69 CE, armies in Egypt proclaimed Vespasian, whom Nero had put in charge of crushing the rebellion in Judaea, to be emperor. Just a few days later, Vespasian's soldiers in Caesarea Maritima, the Roman capital of Judaea, also proclaimed him emperor. The governor of Syria, Gaius Licinius Mucianus, lent his support and his legions to Vespasian's bid for imperial power. Mucianus marched toward Rome to enforce Vespasian's claim, while Vespasian left his son, Titus, in command of operations in Judaea, which included the siege of Jerusalem; Vespasian traveled to Egypt to join the armies there and to secure the empire's grain supply. The city of Rome, which had a population of more than a million people, a staggering number for the ancient world (no European city would surpass that population number until nineteenth-century London), depended on regular shipments of grain from the province of Egypt. Legions on the Roman frontier along the Danube River soon also offered support for Vespasian and began moving toward Rome. Those legions met Vitellius's forces at Bedriacum on October 24, where Vitellius had defeated Otho earlier in the year. Nonetheless, fortune did not favor Vitellius in battle this time, for his army was badly defeated, and the Danubian legions loyal to Vespasian soon marched on Rome. Vitellius found few friends in the capital after his defeat. When forces loyal to Vespasian entered the city, they caught and executed Vitellius. The city suffered some damage in the partisan fighting between factions loyal to Vespasian and to Vitellius. The great Temple of Jupiter Optimus Maximus on the Capitoline Hill, the most important temple in the city of Rome, was burned to the ground as a result of the conflict.[12]

Vespasian: A New Dynasty and a New Rome

In the summer of 70 CE, Vespasian first entered the city of Rome as its emperor (figure 1.3). Vespasian, 60 years of age when he became emperor, was from the Flavian family; he had no familial relationship with the Julio-Claudian dynasty that had ruled the Roman Empire for nearly a hundred years since Augustus had become its first emperor in 27 BCE. But, unlike Galba, Otho, and Vitellius before him, Vespasian successfully retained possession of imperial power until his natural death in 79 CE and established the Flavian dynasty; his elder son, Titus, would rule from 79 to 81 CE and his younger son, Domitian, after Titus's death, would rule from 81 to 96 CE (figures 1.4–1.5).[13]

Ancient authors present Vespasian as a pragmatic, modest, just, and capable ruler, with a quick wit and a fondness for toilet humor. He also possessed great military distinction; in addition to overseeing Roman operations during the Jewish Revolt, he had played a role in Claudius's invasion of Britain in 43 CE and had governed the Roman province of Africa. Despite these qualities that commended him to the reins of the Roman Empire, Vespasian lacked familial legitimacy through a connection with the Julio-Claudian emperors. Therefore, much of his early political program, and the courtiers around him, made ideological connections with the "good" emperors of the Julio-Claudian dynasty, especially the Deified Augustus and the Deified Claudius. To judge from the imagery on their coinage, it appears that attempts had earlier been made to

Figure 1.3. Portrait bust of the emperor Vespasian (Rome, Museo Nazionale Romano alle Terme di Diocleziano, Inv. 330. DAI Fotothek, R. Sansaini, Neg. D-DAI-Rom 54.797)

connect the public presentation of Galba, Otho, and Vitellius with the Julio-Claudian past, especially the Deified Augustus. Before Vespasian even entered Rome, the Senate had invoked the names of Tiberius (14–37 CE) and Claudius in their decree investing him with imperial power in the mode of Augustus (the *Lex de Imperio Vespasiani*), illustrating the necessity of Julio-Claudian precedents for the legitimacy of the new emperor.

When Vespasian arrived in Rome, he found a city in dire need of attention. Rome still bore scars from the Great Fire of 64 CE. The city had sustained further damage from partisan fighting in 69 CE, which had destroyed the great

Figure 1.4. Portrait bust of the emperor Titus (Rome, Vatican Museums—Museo Pio Clementino, Sala dei Busti, Inv. 721. DAI Fotothek, K. Anger, Neg. D-DAI-Rom 96Va.1963)

Temple of Jupiter Optimus Maximus on the Capitoline Hill. Although Vespasian and Titus brought back more wealth and spoils from Judaea after the subjugation of the province and the sacking of the Temple in Jerusalem than Rome had seen since the annexation of Egypt after the Battle of Actium in 31 BCE, Vespasian, instead of using the proceeds to stabilize Rome's finances, used this financial windfall to pay for his extensive building program, which had the Colosseum as its centerpiece.

Roman conquerors traditionally and customarily used spoils from foreign wars to fund public building and largess to the people rather than to ensure the financial stability of the state. Therefore, Vespasian still needed to raise funds

Figure 1.5. Portrait bust of the emperor Domitian (Toledo Museum of Art, Gift of Edward Drummond Libbey, and from the Florence Scott Libbey Bequest in Memory of her Father, Maurice A. Scott, 1990.30)

after the civil war to reorganize the empire and to rebuild certain parts of the city. He instituted a tax on the Jews, whereby Jews who had previously paid an annual tax for the maintenance of the Temple in Jerusalem, which Titus's soldiers had destroyed, were now expected to pay that tax instead to Rome for the reconstruction and upkeep of the Temple of Jupiter Optimus Maximus.[14] This, of course, was a humiliation aimed at the defeated population after the destruction of their temple at the hands of the Romans. Vespasian also reinstituted a tax on the sale of human urine that had been in place under Nero. In Rome, people about the city urinated in ceramic pots along the streets. Slaves collected these pots and emptied them into cesspools. The urine was sold to fullers, who used human urine in the industrial processing of woolen garments, and to others who had industrial purposes for it. In a famous episode, Titus was disgusted that his father would tax the sale of urine, and so Vespasian held a coin to his son's nose and asked him if it smelled. When Titus replied, "No," Vespasian said, "And yet it comes from piss!"[15] Owing to Vespasian's reinstitution of this tax, the word for a public urinal in modern Italian is *vespasiano* and in French it is *vespasienne*. The story of the urine tax illustrates Vespasian's disposition and fondness for toilet humor but also his ingenuity to raise necessary funds for the betterment of the city and the state.

With the funds that he was able to raise, Vespasian set about rebuilding parts of the city that sustained damage in the civil wars and that still suffered from the fire of 64 CE. He completed the reconstruction of a grander Temple of Jupiter Optimus Maximus on the Capitoline Hill in 75 CE.[16] Like many Flavian building projects, the restored temple appeared on the coinage. Much of the rest of Vespasian's urban building program and its associated political art was a response to Nero and promoted Flavian legitimacy and dynastic politics.[17] To support his sprawling palace and its lavish waterworks, Nero had diverted two aqueducts, the Aqua Claudia and the Aqua Anio Novus, which his predecessor, Claudius, had built. Inscriptions of both Vespasian and Titus appear on the Porta Maggiore, a monumentalized section of the Aqua Claudia in Rome that passes over a road, and commemorate their restoration of the aqueduct to public use, acknowledging the Deified Claudius.[18] The focus of Vespasian's building program in Rome was the area to the east of the Forum Romanum, especially the Caelian Hill, the Esquiline Hill, and the valley between those two hills where the Colosseum would be built. The Great Fire of 64 CE had devastated these areas, allowing Nero to build important sections of his Domus Aurea here (compare figure 1.1 with figure 1.6).

Little survives of the Domus Aurea today. The Flavian emperors dismantled much of it after Nero's death and built over it in order to erase his mark on the city and to promote their own dynasty.[19] The architects employed for the construction of the Domus Aurea were Severus and Celer.[20] Pliny the Elder relates that a famous artist, Famulus, painted the interior walls of the Domus Aurea for just a few hours a day and took his craft so seriously that he always painted in a *toga*, which today might be somewhat analogous to painting in a suit and tie or in a tuxedo.[21] Well-preserved remnants of fresco paintings are extant in the Esquiline and Oppian sections of the palace. Renaissance artists studied these paintings and explored the ruins of the Domus Aurea; the paintings had a noticeable influence on Raphael, which is particularly visible in some of his paintings in the rooms of the Vatican palace, such as the loggia of Cardinal

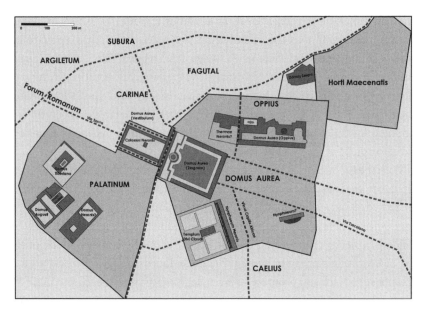

Figure 1.6. The area of the Domus Aurea in the reign of Nero. The *stagnum* is the location upon which the Colosseum was built in the reign of Vespasian. (Cristiano64/Wikimedia Commons)

Bibbiena. The area where these paintings survive is also the best-preserved architecture of the Domus Aurea, just northeast of the present location of the Colosseum, and includes an octagonal room capped by a concrete dome pierced by an *oculus*, a circular opening at the apex of the dome that illuminated the room. This feature illustrates how far Roman facility with concrete construction had advanced and is a precursor to the much grander and more sophisticated concrete dome that would later cap the Pantheon, completed in circa 125 CE in the reign of Hadrian (117–138 CE).

The palace was vast, stretching from the Palatine Hill to the Esquiline Hill, with its core in the Colosseum valley, where a grand fountain house (*nymphaeum*) fed a great lake (figure 1.6). The *nymphaeum* was built into the podium of the languishing Temple of the Deified Claudius. The sprawling palace included gardens and landscaping. The slopes of the surrounding hills, the Caelian Hill, the Velian Hill, the Oppian Hill, and the Esquiline Hill, played host to various complexes of buildings. Construction began on the Palatine Hill early in Nero's reign, before the fire, and expanded when the catastrophe allowed an opportunity for it. Since the ancient literary sources probably embellish the scope of the complex and much of it has not been excavated or was destroyed by Flavian construction, modern scholars disagree on its size. Most suggest that Nero's palace occupied around 200 acres of prime real estate in downtown Rome. Suetonius ascribes a gibe to Nero's lifetime: "Rome is becoming one house; off with you to Veii, Quirites [citizens]! If that house does not soon seize upon Veii as well."[22] Nero's Domus Aurea was also more than a complex of buildings; it included fields, pools, and woods. Suetonius provides a fantastic description of Nero's Domus Aurea:

He made a palace extending all the way from the Palatine to the Esquiline, what at first he called the House of Passage [Domus Transitoria], but when it was burned shortly after its completion and rebuilt, the Golden House. Its size and splendour will be sufficiently indicated by the following details. Its vestibule was large enough to contain a colossal statue of the emperor a hundred and twenty feet high; and it was so extensive that it had a triple colonnade a mile long. There was a pond too, like a sea, surrounded with buildings to represent cities, besides tracts of country, varied by tilled fields, vineyards, pastures and woods, with great numbers of wild and domestic animals. In the rest of the house all parts were overlaid with gold and adorned with gems and mother-of-pearl. There were dining rooms with fretted ceilings of ivory, whose panels could turn and shower down flowers and were fitted with pipes for sprinkling the guests with perfumes. The main banquet hall was circular and constantly revolved day and night, like the heavens. He had baths supplied with sea water and sulphur water. When the edifice was finished in this style and he dedicated it, he deigned to say nothing more in the way of approval than that he was at last beginning to be housed like a human being.[23]

The formal entryway (*vestibulum*) to the Domus Aurea was on the Velian Hill, to the northeast of the Forum Romanum (see figure 1.6). This is presently the area of the Temple of Venus and Roma that Hadrian completed in circa 135 CE, and that is immediately west of the Colosseum today (see figure 3.1). In the *vestibulum*, the architect Zenodorus began work on a colossal bronze statue of Nero that would rise in height to between 103 and 120 Roman feet (approximately 100 to 117 feet, or 30.5 to 36.5 meters); it was thus of similar size to New York's Statue of Liberty, minus the base.[24] The illustrated reconstruction (figure 1.7), based on ancient sources and representations, shows the statue wearing a radiate crown in the manner of Sol (the sun god). The statue also holds a rudder on a globe, an attribute of the goddess Fortuna (Fortune) that suggests guidance or good administration, and leans on a column. Nero is also nude, a convention in Greek art, and often adopted in Roman art, to signify heroism

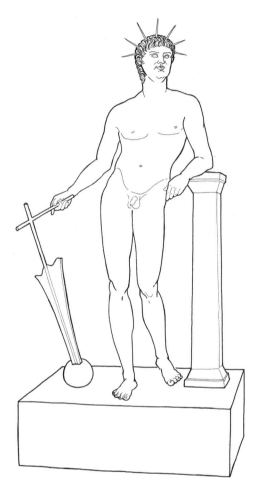

Figure 1.7. Reconstruction of the Colossus of Nero (Drawing by S. Bertolin, reproduced with the permission of Marianne Bergmann)

or divinity. The colossal statue was incomplete at the time of Nero's death, but Vespasian finished it with alterations so that it portrayed Sol rather than Nero, and it became known as the Colossus of Sol.[25] The rays on the statue's head were 23.5 Roman feet in length (just under 23 feet, or approximately 7 meters).

Beyond the *vestibulum* and the Colossus was a great artificial lake (*stagnum*) (figure 1.6). To its south, the grand fountain house, built into the podium of the Temple of the Deified Claudius, replenished the lake. Construction on the Temple of the Deified Claudius had begun at Agrippina's command shortly after

Claudius's death, but Nero never completed it and apparently had little interest in the realization of Claudius's temple or his cult. Vespasian would ultimately complete that temple.

Although ancient writers under the Flavians, and beyond, condemned the excesses and scale of Nero's Domus Aurea, it seems that what really peeved these aristocratic authors was how it functioned and what it did. After all, previous emperors had built large palaces and had large estates outside of the city. Hadrian's villa at Tivoli, which did not attract the ire of Roman authors, would be approximately the same size as Nero's Domus Aurea.[26] Although functioning as private residences, elite Roman houses were also semipublic. At Pompeii, for instance, visitors today will see benches outside these homes or in the *vestibulum* where clients would wait before they were allowed to enter the *atrium* to greet their elite patron, who would stand beyond the reflecting pool inside the *atrium*, the first and main room of a Roman house. Elite Romans conducted business in their homes, and so did the emperors. Pliny also states that Nero rebuilt the Temple of Fortune within the bounds of his Domus Aurea, which makes little sense if the Domus Aurea was an entirely private palace complex.[27] Indeed, Nero's Domus Aurea is an elite Roman house on a massive scale; the pool in the *atrium* of his house was the same size as the footprint of the Colosseum, which later replaced it.

Since the time of the Republic, wealthy Romans had built public gardens on the edge of the city for the enjoyment of the common people. Nero's palace brought the countryside into the heart of the city with its lake, fountains, and gardens. Nero was also a populist ruler who actively cultivated the affections of the common people. The general public could enter parts of his palace, and it gave them a certain level of access to the emperor. The Domus Aurea subverted traditional Roman social order by providing a place for public enjoyment and leisure in downtown Rome, just next door to the Forum Romanum, which was home to the Senate and the center of government. This fomented the resentment of the senatorial nobility toward Nero.

This area of the Domus Aurea (adjacent to the eastern end of the Forum Romanum) was the major focus of Vespasian's building program. In literature of the Flavian era, attacks on the palace characterized it as a sprawling home for a monarch's personal pleasure, downplaying the evident public aspects of the Domus Aurea. An epigram by Martial in praise of the Flavians relates the apparent aim of the new regime's building in this area, as important components of the Domus Aurea were dismantled and the space made available for different types of public buildings:

Here, where the starry colossus sees the constellations close at hand and a lofty framework rises in the middle of the road, the hated halls of a cruel king used to gleam and in the whole city there was only one house standing. Here, where the awesome bulk of the amphitheatre soars before our eyes, once lay Nero's pools. Here, where we marvel at the swift blessings of the baths, an arrogant estate had robbed the poor of their dwellings. Where the Claudian portico weaves its spreading shade marks the point at which the palace finally stopped. Rome has been restored to herself, and with you in charge, Caesar, what used to be the pleasure of a master is now the pleasure of the people.[28]

If we take the passage at face value, Nero confiscated land formerly occupied by the homes of the poor in order to build a lavish palace for himself. This assertion may well be an invention of post-Neronian elites in the concoction of Flavian public ideology. The neighboring Palatine Hill had long been an elite district. A significant portion of the Esquiline Hill was composed of public parks, such as the Gardens of Maecenas, while other parts of the hill were home to Rome's middle class and elites. Even in the Colosseum valley, which Suetonius says was a commercial district before the fire, excavations revealed an aristocratic house before the Great Fire of 64 CE. The area that Nero appropriated for the Domus Aurea thus seems to have been taken not from Rome's poor but perhaps instead from Rome's wealthy and noble classes, also explaining why the palace complex was so loathed by (aristocratic) Roman authors.[29] The sorts of buildings and houses that populated the area prior to the fire of 64 CE are, however, a subject of ongoing debate and speculation, as there are few archaeological remains that predate the palace. When his Domus Aurea became something of a public amusement park for the common people, subverting Roman sensibilities regarding social distinctions and physical separations among the classes, it may have further incited their hostility toward Nero. Rather than returning the land to the original owners, Vespasian's building program here sought to maintain the area for public use through the construction of several public buildings that promoted the new regime and its political ideology (see chapter 3). At the center of the building program was the Colosseum, which came to rest on what was Nero's great lake, and which was a public building for the enjoyment of all, although it reasserted social order through its strict segregation of classes in its seating arrangements.

Even though most of the monuments discussed in this book, and the Colosseum itself, were Vespasian's vision, he died in 79 CE and did not live to see the full realization of his plan for Rome, or the dedication of his new amphitheater.

It was left to Titus to dedicate the Colosseum the following year in 80 CE, to-gether with the Baths of Titus, just to the north of the Colosseum. Neverthe-less, the amphitheater was incomplete during the inaugural games; it certainly did not yet have the substructures that enhanced the spectacles by allowing gladiators, animals, and scenery to be transported to the arena floor from be-low. Under Titus, the highest level was probably of wooden construction, if pres-ent at all. The last of the Flavian emperors, Domitian, completed the amphi-theater. He added the substructures and finished the Colosseum to its fourth level. His reign saw the completion of other monuments in the area around the Colosseum, including a triumphal arch dedicated to his deified brother at the eastern end of the Forum Romanum, the Meta Sudans fountain immediately to the southwest of the Colosseum, and gladiatorial schools to the east and south of the amphitheater. The Colosseum was truly a dynastic monument, for each of the Flavian emperors played a role in shaping what the Colosseum was and what it and their monuments in the area said about the political image of the imperial family.

-II-

A Modern Amphitheater in Ancient Rome

TODAY, WE KNOW THE great amphitheater in the center of Rome as the Colosseum (figures 2.1–2.3), but that is not what the Romans called it.[1] Another popular term for it in scholarly literature is the "Flavian Amphitheater" (Amphitheatrum Flavium), although there is no evidence that this is how the Romans referred to the building either. The reconstruction of the dedicatory inscription from the amphitheater posits the "New Amphitheater" (Amphitheatrum Novum); Martial, the contemporary poet, called it simply the "amphitheater" (*amphitheatrum*) in his *Book of Spectacles*, as did Suetonius writing some decades later.[2] A fragmentary marble plan of the city of Rome, known as the Forma Urbis Romae, which dates from the early third century CE in the reign of Septimius Severus (193–211 CE), contains an incomplete section for the Colosseum and some surrounding buildings, such as the Ludus Magnus, a gladiator school to its east.[3] In the fragments of the plan for the Colosseum, remnants of the inscribed label read "ATRUM," which can be reconstructed as "[AMPHITHE]ATRVM" (figure 2.4). As the Colosseum was the only functional amphitheater in Rome at the time of its construction, it is probable that it was simply referred to as the "amphitheater," as sources such as Martial and the marble plan indicate. People began to call the amphitheater the "Colosseum" only in the Middle Ages. The term may derive from the Colossus of Sol (formerly the Colossus of Nero, figure 1.7), which the emperor Hadrian moved next to the amphitheater circa 128 CE to make room for his construction of the Temple of Venus and Roma, or from the colossal dimensions of the amphitheater itself.[4] The Colosseum was among the most advanced buildings in Rome at the time of its construction, in terms of engineering, scale, and resources invested in its realization; the amenities it provided spectators were not dissimilar to what modern spectators expect at stadiums and sporting arenas today. A building of the scale and complexity of the Colosseum required great expense, organization, and the deployment of a massive force of specialists, paid workmen, and slave labor. In modern literature on the Colosseum, one often reads the glib statement that Jewish slaves, taken after the Jewish Revolt, built the Colosseum. In fact, there is no ancient evidence that Jewish slaves were compelled to build the amphitheater; it is, nonetheless, quite possible and commensurate with Roman practice, for forcing Jewish slaves to build a structure paid for by the looting of sacred objects from their temple would heap humiliation upon defeat.[5] In addition to the massive force of unskilled labor needed to build the Colosseum, there would have also been a large team of engineers, architects, supervisors, professional sculptors, and craftsmen.

The Façade and Plan

Roman amphitheaters have an elliptical footprint, as exhibited in the fragments of the Forma Urbis Romae that depict the floor plan of the Colosseum.[6] This shape increased visibility for spectators. The type of structure that we know as an amphitheater had existed since the Roman Republic, although in those days Romans called an amphitheater a *spectacula*, the same word used for the spectacles that occurred in the venue. In the city of Rome and elsewhere, these were temporary wooden structures, erected for games and festivals and then disassembled until needed again. The first stone amphitheaters were built in Italy in the first century BCE, although wooden amphitheaters continued to be built through the first century CE. Wooden amphitheaters were erected in the Forum Romanum during the Republic, as attested by surviving archaeological evidence and architectural features, including substructures (*hypogea*) and bases for capstans (vertical beams equipped with perpendicular handles that could be pushed by slaves or workers) that powered elevators to the arena floor. The elliptical shape of stone amphitheaters, like the Colosseum, may have derived from wooden amphitheaters constructed in the Forum Romanum that, by necessity, were built that way when constructed in the rectangular open area between the Basilica Aemilia and the Basilica Sempronia.[7] The word *amphitheatrum* appears to have entered the Latin language in the age of Augustus and derives from the Greek terms *amphi*, meaning "both sides," and *theatrum* (*theatron* in Greek), meaning a theater or, more literally, a "seeing-place." Thus, it refers to a double theater, or a place where one can see from multiple angles.[8]

The Colosseum's ground plan forms two axes (figure 2.5). The long axis is the imaginary line that runs through the center of the ellipse at its longest point, while the short axis passes through the middle of the ellipse at its widest point; the two axes cross in the exact middle of the arena floor. The Colosseum measures 185 meters (609 feet) in length on the long axis and 154 meters (505 feet) wide along the short axis. After Nero's great lake was drained and approximately 30,000 tons of dirt were excavated, workers poured a concrete ring as the foundation upon which the bulk of the amphitheater sits.

At the three lowest levels above ground, there are two tall, annular passageways with intersecting radial passages that lead to entrances and exits (figures 2.6–2.8). These ambulatories are also visible from the exterior today when looking at the amphitheater from the southeast or southwest, since an earthquake in September 1349 caused the collapse of the vaults and façade wall on that side and exposed them. Looking from the south, one can see where the tunnels continue into the surviving parts of the superstructure on the northern side. There are two additional ambulatories in the first level, plus a service corridor under the podium, a third ambulatory on the second level, and just one ambulatory on the fourth level (figures 2.7–2.8).

The outer walls and piers were made of travertine, a form of limestone common in Italy. Scholars estimate that approximately 100,000 cubic meters of travertine were quarried at Tivoli, in the hills east of Rome, to provide building material for the Colosseum. Arches and barrel vaults of brick-faced concrete join the travertine piers, and it was on the tops of these that the seats for the spectators (the *cavea*) were placed and upon which the amphitheater's great mass rests. In addition to the heavy use of travertine in the Colosseum's piers, outer rings, and façade, brick-faced concrete is used more heavily nearer the arena floor and for walls in the inner passageways.[9]

The Colosseum is 48.5 meters (159 feet) tall, approximately the same height as a modern 15-story building. The best-preserved section of the Colosseum's façade is along the northern side (figure 2.9). The façade of the outer wall on the southern side, and the two vaults behind it, collapsed after the earthquake in 1349. Throughout the building, visitors today will see pockmarks in the stone surfaces, especially where stones join together. In the Middle Ages, people chiseled into the stones to extract the iron clamps that the Romans used to lock the stones into place. The removal of these clamps probably weakened the façade and vaults on the southern side, facilitating its collapse in 1349, after which the fallen stones were quarried for building projects in Rome, including St. Peter's Basilica on Vatican Hill. In 1805 Pope Pius VII was responsible for restorations to the Colosseum that, among other things, reinforced the weakened arches and vaults on that side and prevented further collapse by building two large brick supports on the remaining ends of the façade and the second annular vault. Pope Pius IX commanded additional reinforcements to prevent the amphitheater's collapse in 1852. These abutments are still visible today, as is the inscription marking Pope Pius IX's work on the western side over the modern reinforcements (figure 2.1).

Four horizontal sections characterize the Colosseum's façade (figure 2.10). At the lowest level of the façade, 80 arched entrances pierce the building. Roman numerals appear above each entrance on the exterior façade wall; the numbers presumably corresponded with tickets held by spectators to guide them to their appropriate seating sections (figure 2.11). The entrance that survives on the northern side of the short axis lacks a number, suggesting that it was a special entrance. In all probability, the corresponding entrance on the southern side of the short axis, as well as the entrances on the ends of the long axis that no longer survive, also were unnumbered. Each of these was a special entrance and not for the use of the general public. The entryways on the short axis led directly to viewing platforms at the central edge of the arena floor, giving those spectators the best seats with the best views, the modern equivalent of the "50-yard-line seats" at an American football game, or the seats adjacent to the halfway line in a European football (soccer) game. Certainly, the emperor and his entourage occupied one of these seating platforms, while the occupants of the opposite viewing box have been the subject of some speculation and little critical inquiry until recently. The two entrances on either side of the long axis led directly to the arena floor and thus would not have been used by spectators. The western entrance is conventionally referred to as the Porta Triumphalis, through which the procession that preceded a day of games would enter the arena, while the eastern entrance is called the Porta Libitinensis, after Libitina (a goddess of funerals), through which the dead were removed from the arena. We do not know, however, through which of these entrances the procession entered or through which the dead were removed. Between the entrances along the façade at ground level are engaged Tuscan columns—that is, columns that are attached (engaged) to the wall but project out from the surface. Tuscan-style columns are a native Italic column, similar to Doric columns in Greek architecture.

Above the entrances at ground level are two successive levels of arcades (figures 2.10–2.11). Engaged Ionic columns appear between the arcades on the second level, whereas engaged Corinthian columns delineate the arcades on the third level. Ancient representations also show statues filling the arcades on the second and third levels, as on coins struck under the emperor Titus, who dedicated the Colosseum in 80 CE, on virtually identical coins of Domitian struck in honor of the Deified Titus in circa 81/82 CE (figure 2.12), and on a relief from the Tomb of the Haterii, which dates to the early second century CE (figure 2.13). At the uppermost level (also called the attic level) of the Colosseum, alternating above each arcade on the third level, is either a flat wall or a square window (figures 2.9–2.10); between every section and above the columns of the third level is a Corinthian pilaster (a pilaster is also attached to the wall but is flat and in low relief, unlike an engaged column). As is visible on the coins depicting the Colosseum, large bronze shields decorated the flat areas between the windows on this level (figure 2.12). In each section above the area of the shields and windows are three pedestals that project out from the façade wall and that supported wooden masts that passed through corresponding sockets in the entablature that crowns the very top of the building (the entablature is the horizontal lintel above the pilasters that caps the top of the Colosseum) (figures 2.10–2.11 and 2.14). The masts that sat on the pedestals, locked in place by the sockets in the entablature, anchored the amphitheater's awnings (reconstructions in figures 2.2–2.3 show the masts in position; the coins, figure 2.12, also show masts at the top of the amphitheater). This upward progression of architectural orders in amphitheater façades first appeared in the Colosseum, although theater façades had had similar arrangements for a long time. After its construction, this use and organization of the various architectural orders in the Colosseum inspired the decoration of amphitheater façades in Italy outside of Rome and in the provinces, as at Arelate (modern Arles, France) and also at Thysdrus (modern El Djem, Tunisia), where arcades are placed above arched entryways that pierce the façade, and where between each arch and arcade an upward progression of orders of engaged columns or pilasters appears.

According to ancient representations, statues filled the arcades of the Colosseum's façade on the second and third levels. The bronze coins of Titus and Domitian from 80 and 81/82 CE, respectively, depict the central entrance, elaborated in the form of a triumphal arch, and what presumably is one of the main entrances on the short axis that led to a viewing platform on the arena's edge (figure 2.12). Above that is a *quadriga* (a four-horse chariot) driven by a figure who must be the emperor. The relief from the Tomb of the Haterii similarly depicts an elaborated entrance in the form of a triumphal arch surmounted by a *quadriga* (figure 2.13). A surviving travertine block in front of an engaged column on the entrance to the viewing platform on the short axis of the northern side further suggests that the entrance was built out in an elaborated form (figure 2.15), and a ruined concrete base in the arcade above that entrance may have been for the core of the chariot group (see the base above the central, axial entrance in figure 2.10). This archaeological evidence proves that this entrance was monumentalized, as attested by the coins and the relief from the Tomb of the Haterii.[10]

These two pieces of visual evidence, and the travertine block on the northern side, allow us to reconstruct the two entrances on opposite sides of the short axis as styled as triumphal arches, complete with the triumphant symbolism of a *quadriga*, which customarily carried the emperor during triumphal parades in Rome after a major military victory. The entrances on the opposite sides of the long axis may well have been elaborated in this form also, for the Flavian amphitheater at Puteoli, on the Bay of Naples, which was greatly influenced by the form and decoration of the Colosseum, bears evidence that its four axial entrances were elaborated in the form of arches (reconstructions in figures 2.2–2.3 show elaborated entrances on the four ends of Colosseum's axes). The symbolism of the entrances styled as triumphal arches, and the shields in its attic level, communicated the Flavian military victory over Judaea, from which the financial proceeds also paid for the construction of the Colosseum according to the building's dedicatory inscription, which states that it was built *ex manubis*—"from the spoils of war."[11]

From the coins, it is virtually impossible to tell who or what the statues in the other arcades portrayed. On the few exceptionally well-preserved specimens of the rare Colosseum coins that still exist, the central arcade above the *quadriga* appears to host a sculpture group with multiple figures (figure 2.12). There is a central element, which resembles a palm tree, with a figure on each side of it. This general layout echoes the imagery on contemporaneous coins that depict a palm tree, symbolic of Judaea, flanked by the victorious emperor and a dejected personification of Judaea or a Jewish captive.[12] The presence of such a statue group here would be consistent with the other triumphant imagery and associations in the Colosseum already noted.

On the relief from the Tomb of the Haterii, statues of Hercules, Apollo, and Aesculapius are depicted within the arcades of the second level and in the third level are statues of eagles (figure 2.13).[13] The eagles might symbolize Jupiter or deified emperors. On the relief, the Colosseum is depicted only to its third level and, of course, in an abbreviated format. Whether the relief depicts any of the statues that were originally displayed in the arcades of the Colosseum is an open question; the presence of Ionic columns between the arches on the first level defies reality. The representation of eagles on the third level contradicts the use of standing figures in this level, as portrayed by the Flavian coins (figure 2.12). William Jensen argues that the selection of the statues of Hercules, Apollo, and Aesculapius refers to the myth of Admetus and Alcestis, which ends in the salvation of Alcestis, because all three of these figures play a central role in the myth; he also notes that the eagles could have symbolized apotheosis. In such an instance, the statues may not have reflected the reality of the sculptural program on the Colosseum's façade but may have been chosen instead to bear on themes of death and afterlife, since the relief in question was part of a tomb for a woman.[14]

Aside from the four sculpture groups above the axial entrances that were *quadrigae*, and any potential sculpture groups showing conqueror and conquered around a palm tree, it is probable that the statues or statue groups within the arcades of the Colosseum's façade, of which there were 160 in total, originally had as their common theme divine retribution and punishment. These would have specifically alluded to the executions staged as mythological enactments that entertained spectators at midday (see chapter 4). Two large sculptures excavated in Puteoli, at an amphitheater built in the Flavian period shortly after the Colosseum's construction and influenced by its design, portray Ixion strapped to the wheel and Prometheus chained to a rock while a bird devours his liver. These mythical figures defied authority, specifically the gods, and were punished eternally for it. In fact, an enactment of a punishment evocative of Prometheus's eternal torment is a mode of execution for a criminal in the Colosseum's earliest games.[15] Similarly, in Capua, to the south of Rome, at another amphitheater built in the Flavian period and influenced by the Colosseum's construction and layout, half of the original marble reliefs survive and primarily depict mythological scenes, especially punishments, such as the Prometheus myth and the flaying of Marsyas, as well as other torments from myth that were theatrically staged as executions according to various ancient sources. Freestanding statues of Greek subjects were also part of the major decorative program.

The message sent by the use of Greek mythological subjects, and especially of punishments that related to executions staged as mythological enactments in the amphitheater, was clear. As figures such as Prometheus, Ixion, and Marsyas defied divine authority, or displayed excessive hubris, they acted as metaphors for those who defied Roman imperial authority and who received their just dues in the amphitheater for subverting the Roman political order.[16]

The sculptural program in the arcades of the Colosseum probably also focused on Greek mythological subjects, and particularly punishments, especially as the Colosseum was the architectural prototype for the amphitheaters at Puteoli and Capua. While the statues depicted in the Colosseum's arcades on the relief from the Tomb of the Haterii may have been chosen for their funerary symbolism, as Jensen argued, they could also have been among the actual statues or statue groups on the Colosseum's façade. Hercules ascended to divinity during his apotheosis when he was burned on a pyre. Tertullian and Lucillius attest the executions of criminals enacted in the guise of this myth.[17] Marsyas was a satyr who challenged Apollo in a musical contest with the flute and lost to the god. To punish him for his arrogance, Apollo bound or nailed him to a tree and flayed him alive. Aesculapius was struck down and killed by Jupiter for defying him and reviving the dead without his consent. The presence of Hercules, Apollo (with regard to his agency in Marsyas's punishment), and Aesculapius among the statues on the Colosseum's façade could have communicated the theme of divine retribution through mythological enactments, for these punishments are of the same sort one reads about in sources such as Martial, Strabo, Tertullian, and Ulpian.

The Colosseum's status by the time of its dedication by Titus in 80 CE has been the subject of debate. As regards the façade and internal structure, the Colosseum may have been completed in stone only to the third level by the time of the first games, and the fourth level may have been constructed in wood during the inauguration, or it may not have been present at all.[18] Domitian, who succeeded his brother in 81 CE, added the fourth level in stone during his reign. Indeed, the Chronographer of 354 CE claims that Domitian completed the Colosseum *ad clypea* ("to the shields"), referring to the shields on the uppermost level of the façade. This suggests that coins struck in the reign of Titus that depict the Colosseum in the year that it was inaugurated and the coins struck early in Domitian's reign (figure 2.12) show the structure as it was anticipated to look when the stone façade would be completed.[19]

In 217 CE, nearly a century and a half after its inauguration, lightning struck the Colosseum, causing it to burn for days.[20] Today, we think of the Colosseum as a massive relic of stone and concrete, largely impervious to fire, but one must remember that the living Colosseum of ancient Rome contained wooden seating and fixtures in its upper levels. There were also the masts, thousands of square meters of linen for its awning, and thousands of meters of rigging to support the awning, not to mention the wooden arena floor and the various wooden components of the substructures that powered the elevators and cages for gladiators and animals to appear on the arena floor. There was thus ample kindling. The extent of the damage was so great that the reconstruction effort was not finished until the reign of Severus Alexander (222–235 CE), although the need for further work after his death is suggested by a medallion of Gordian III from circa 241–244 CE and some other literary sources (see chapter 5 and figure 5.1).

The widespread damage and reconstruction also make it difficult to distinguish between what is Flavian construction and what is later reconstruction. Nevertheless, thanks to a very detailed study by Lynne Lancaster, an archaeologist specializing in Roman engineering and building techniques, we now understand that the Severan reconstruction was present not only in the upper levels, as earlier believed, but extended also down to the vaults of the ground level and heavily affected the northwestern quadrant of the Colosseum.[21] There is significantly more Severan reconstruction work at the uppermost levels and less on the ground level, which is consistent with the lightning strike and consequent conflagration described by Cassius Dio, an author who was contemporary with the cataclysm and eyewitness to it. The outer ambulatories on the Colosseum's northern side on the first three levels from bays numbered 34 to 60 are Severan reconstruction (refer to figure 2.5 for the numbering of entrances); the outer wall of the façade from the east end to bay number 40 is original Flavian work. The worst of the damage in 217 CE was between bays 40 and 47; that entire section of the façade is Severan reconstruction.

Visitors to the Colosseum with Lancaster's research in hand might be able to distinguish for themselves between original Flavian construction, Severan reconstruction, and modern work. For instance, Flavian brickwork uses thin bricks with thin mortar joints, raked by a trowel; Severan brickwork incorporates thin bricks with thick mortar joints, not raked by a trowel. Modern reconstructions and reinforcements generally use much thicker bricks. Flavian concrete incorporates *tufo giallo*, yellow tufa (tufa is a porous rock commonly used in construction in ancient Rome), whereas Severan concrete uses *tufo lionato*, a tawny-colored tufa, which is a darker orange-to-brown color.

Ancient vaults have visible gouge marks on their surfaces, as these prepared the surface for a coat of plaster; in fact, in many sections of the Colosseum, visitors will see remnants of ancient plaster. Vaults reconstructed in the modern era generally have smooth surfaces, because they were never intended to receive a plaster veneer. On the interior of the highest level of the Colosseum, one can see evidence of Severan or post-Severan reconstruction through the incorporation of *spolia* (reused building materials) in the construction of the façade wall (figure 2.16).

The Awning (*Velarium*)

Just as some modern sports stadiums have retractable roofs, such as AT&T Stadium (formerly Cowboys Stadium) in Arlington, Texas, or Wembley Stadium in London, Roman theaters and amphitheaters were often outfitted with retractable awnings to shade spectators from heat and the glare of the sun and perhaps also to protect them against light inclement weather.[22] These retractable awnings are known as a *velaria* or *vela* (singular: *velarium*; *velum*). The use of the *velarium* in the Colosseum was, therefore, not an innovation, although the awning was no doubt the most extensive and complex awning system in the Roman world. Textual sources indicate that awnings had provided shade to spectators at shows since at least 69 BCE, a century and a half before the Colosseum's dedication; Julius Caesar provided awnings for gladiatorial games in the wooden amphitheater constructed in the Forum Romanum in 46 BCE.[23] In a passage alleging several gratuitous cruelties that the emperor Caligula (37–41 CE) inflicted upon spectators in the Circus Maximus, theaters, and the amphitheater, Suetonius says that he would sometimes command the retraction of the awning in the amphitheater during gladiatorial shows at the hottest part of the day and forbid anyone to leave.[24] We may assume that the venue in question was the Augustan-era Amphitheater of Statilius Taurus.

The expense of providing awnings in amphitheaters was undertaken by the sponsor of games and was so important that their provision was listed alongside the spectacles in painted advertisements that survive at Pompeii. Visitors today can easily pick out the phrase *vela erunt* in many of the surviving advertisements, which translates "there will be awnings." Painted on the house of Trebius Valens at Pompeii, for example, is an advertisement that reads, "At the dedication [Ocella] of the *opus tabularum* of Gnaeus Alleius Nigidius Maius, at Pompeii on 13 June, there will be a procession, hunt, athletics, and awnings."[25] At the Colosseum, the awning would have been a luxury paid for by the emperor.

The awning was a spectacle in and of itself, on account of the elaborate rigging system in the Colosseum and the vibrant colors used for the cloth. Before the Colosseum's construction, the poet Lucretius described theaters with yellow, red, and purple awnings that cast colored shadows upon the spectators therein; Pliny and Cassius Dio say that Nero had used dark-blue awnings that imitated the night sky, decorated with stars to heighten the effect.[26]

As mentioned earlier in this chapter, on the northern façade of the Colosseum one can see three pedestals in each section between the pilasters in the highest level, above the windows or flat areas where the bronze shields were once affixed; corresponding with the pedestals are sockets in the entablature at the very top of the amphitheater (figures 2.10, 2.11, and 2.14). Each pedestal and socket locked into place an individual wooden mast. There would have originally been eighty of these sections, as each section sits above the arcades and entrances below. Thus, the Colosseum had 240 wooden masts at the very top of the Colosseum that supported an elaborate web of rigging from which the various sections of the awning were deployed (figure 2.17). Presumably, there was a ring of ropes suspended over the area of the arena floor so that the awning would form an *oculus* that would allow unfiltered light to illuminate the spectacles in the center of the arena.

Although the exact method for the rigging and deployment of the *velarium* is a debated topic, some scholars once believed that the lines were further anchored at ground level with ropes that ran from the masts at the top to upright stones at ground level that encircled the Colosseum's façade wall. It is now understood, and more universally accepted, that these stones supported bars and chains between them to cordon off the Colosseum from wheeled traffic, making the space between the Colosseum and the stones a pedestrian zone. The fact that the stones are not embedded into a foundation but held down only by their own weight supports the logic of this interpretation, as they would need to be sturdier if they anchored the ropes at ground level. Today, one can see five of these upright stones still in their original position on the northeastern side of the Colosseum (figure 2.18). Each stone has holes that supported bars and a hole at the top to support a chain. Those who have wished to reconstruct these as anchors for the rigging of the *velarium* posited cranks on these stones.

Inside the Colosseum, there are remains of stairways against the interior of the façade wall at the highest level that would have allowed workers to service the masts and the web of rigging. As sailors and marines were experienced with masts, rigging, and sails on ships (analogous to the system of awnings deployed from masts and ropes), they were enlisted to control and maintain awnings in the Colosseum and other spectacle buildings in the city of Rome. These hundreds of men camped at the Castra Misenatum in Rome, which tells us that they were marines from Misenum, the naval base of the imperial fleet located on the Bay of Naples.[27]

Figure 2.1. The western side of the Colosseum viewed on its long axis. The façade and vaults to the south (*right*) collapsed in the earthquake of 1349; the northern side (*left*) is more complete. The brick abutments at the ends of the surviving walls were added in the nineteenth century to forestall further collapse of the façade and vaults. A papal inscription below a cross marks the work. (Photograph: Nathan T. Elkins, 2017)

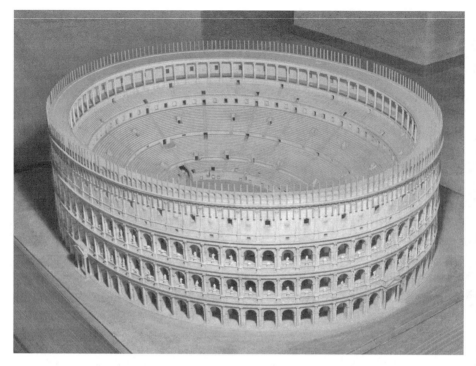

Figure 2.2. Model of the reconstructed Colosseum (Rome, Museo della Civiltà Romana. DAI Fotothek, Neg. D-DAI-Rom 73.1000)

Figure 2.3. A digitally reconstructed view of the Colosseum from the terrace of the Temple of the Deified Claudius (to the southeast of the amphitheater), placing the Meta Sudans (the conical fountain) to its left and the Baths of Titus behind it and to its right. The Temple of Venus and Roma is to the left of the Colosseum and beyond the Meta Sudans; Domitian's gladiator schools are to the right of the Colosseum. (Image from Virtual Rome, a digital model developed by Dr. Matthew Nicholls, © 2018 University of Reading. Reproduced with permission)

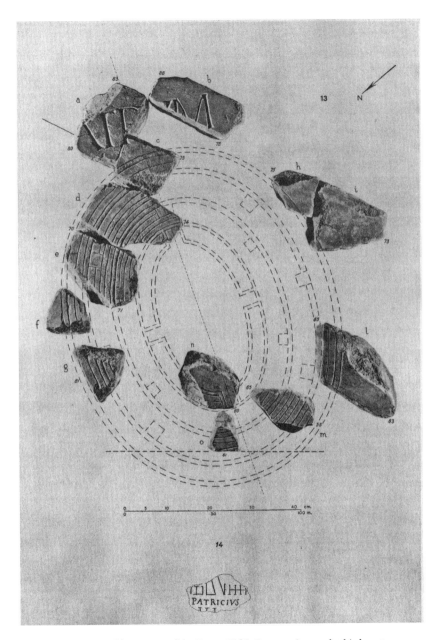

Figure 2.4. A section of fragments of the Forma Urbis Romae, circa early third century CE, depicting the Colosseum, from G. Carettoni, *La pianta marmorea di Roma antica. Forma Urbis Romae* (Rome: Comune di Roma, 1960) pl. 19 (© Roma, Sovrintendenza Capitolina ai Beni Culturali)

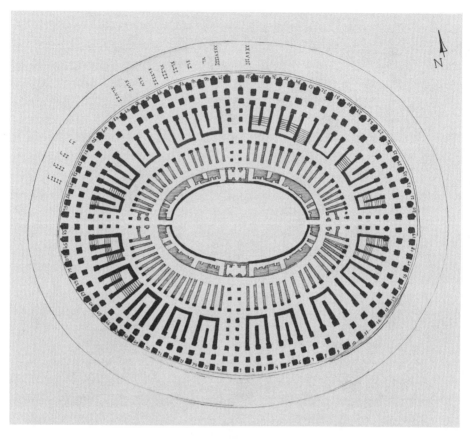

Figure 2.5. Plan of the first level of the Colosseum. Numbers indicate entrances; the outer line indicates the area where vertical stones were placed that demarcated a pedestrian zone around the Colosseum. (Drawing: Cade Kegerreis)

Figure 2.6. The outer ambulatory on the first level of the northern side of the Colosseum (Photograph: Nathan T. Elkins, 2017)

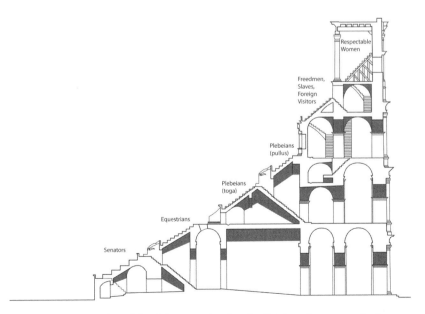

Respectable Women

Freedmen, Slaves, Foreign Visitors

Plebeians (pullus)

Plebeians (toga)

Equestrians

Senators

Figure 2.7. A cross section of the Colosseum showing the division of spectators in the *cavea* and the passageways (Drawing: Lisa Fehsenfeld)

Figure 2.8. Model of the reconstructed Colosseum with a cutaway to show interior passageways beneath the *cavea* (Rome, Museo della Civiltà Romana. DAI Fotothek, Neg. D-DAI-Rom 73.1002)

Figure 2.9. The northern façade of the Colosseum, viewed from the northwest; the square base to the right and in the foreground, where the trees are located, marks the spot to which the Colossus of Sol was moved in circa 128 CE at the command of Hadrian. (Photograph: Nathan T. Elkins, 2017)

Figure 2.10. Detail of the northern façade of the Colosseum on the short axis, showing the engaged Tuscan columns on the first level, Ionic columns on the second, Corinthian columns on the third, and Corinthian pilasters on the fourth. Between pairs of square windows on the fourth level were large bronze shields. Above an inscription of Pope Pius IX (inserted in 1852) on the central axial entrance is a ruined concrete base, perhaps for a chariot group. (Photograph: Nathan T. Elkins, 2017)

Figure 2.11. Detail of entrances inscribed LIII and LIIII (53 and 54) on the northern façade of the Colosseum, with a view of the upper levels, ascending from engaged Tuscan columns on the first level, Ionic on the second, Corinthian on the third, and Corinthian pilasters on the fourth. Note the pedestals and corresponding sockets for the wooden masts at the top of the amphitheater. (Photograph: Nathan T. Elkins, 2017)

Figure 2.12. A bronze coin (*sestertius*) of Domitian from circa 81/82 CE struck for the Deified Titus, depicting on its obverse a view of the Colosseum from the area of the Caelian Hill. On its left is the Meta Sudans and on its right is the *porticus* of the Baths of Titus. The reverse depicts Titus, seated on a curule chair, holding a branch and surrounded by captured weapons from the Jewish Revolt; the text on the reverse translates to "To the Deified Titus Augustus Vespasianus, Son of the Deified Vespasian, by Decree of the Senate" (DIVO AVG T DIVI VESP F VESPASIAN, S C). (Formerly of the J. Campion Coll., and previously *Ars Classica* 13 [June 27–29, 1928], no. 182; image reproduced by permission of Dix Noonan Webb)

Figure 2.13. Detail of the relief from the Tomb of the Haterii showing the Colosseum (Rome, Musei Vaticani-Museo Gregoriano Profano, Inv. 9997. DAI Fotothek, Faraglia, Neg. D-DAI-Rom 34.1623)

Figure 2.14. Detail of a section of the fourth level of the northern façade of the Colosseum showing pedestals and sockets (Photograph: Nathan T. Elkins, 2003)

Figure 2.15. Detail of a travertine block projecting outward from the central northern entrance on the short axis, suggesting the elaboration of the axial entrance (Photograph: Nathan T. Elkins, 2017)

Figure 2.16. Detail of the interior of the upper level of the Colosseum on the northwestern side showing the use of *spolia* in the reconstruction of the travertine façade wall. Note the incorporation of column drums and other architectural blocks. (Photograph: Nathan T. Elkins, 2003)

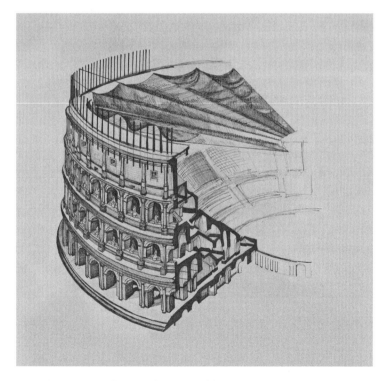

Figure 2.17. Reconstruction drawing of a section of the Colosseum showing the façade, interior passageways, and the *velarium* deployed from wooden masts (Drawing: Cade Kegerreis)

Figure 2.18. A section of five upright stones on the northeastern side of the Colosseum that served as boundary stones to delineate between a pedestrian zone on the Colosseum side and an area for wheeled traffic outside of it; in the past, some have interpreted these stones as anchors at ground level to support and control rigging for the *velarium*. These stones originally formed a perimeter around the Colosseum. (Photograph: Nathan T. Elkins, 2017)

Figure 2.19. An interior view to the east on the long axis of the Colosseum showing the arena floor partially reconstructed in wood. Above are the walls, piers, and vaults that supported the *cavea*; the area of (incorrectly) reconstructed senatorial seating is just to the left of the eastern entrance on the long axis. Below are the substructures, divided into corridors. (Photograph: Nathan T. Elkins, 2008)

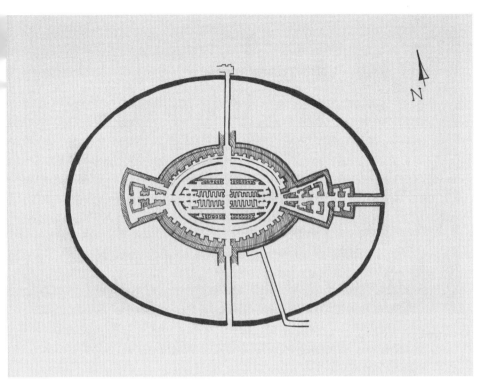

Figure 2.20. Plan of the substructures of the Colosseum. The tunnel that extends to the southeast, emerging from the Colosseum's outer perimeter, is the so-called Cryptoporticus of Commodus. (Drawing: Cade Kegerreis)

Figure 2.21. A view of the northern platform from the northern passageway on the short axis. This is the probable location of the imperial viewing box, where Mussolini's cross sits. (Photograph: Nathan T. Elkins, 2017)

Figure 2.22. A silver coin (*denarius*) of Titus from 80 CE depicting on its obverse a portrait of Titus and his imperial titles, which continue on the reverse. The reverse depicts a draped seat surmounted by a winged thunderbolt. (Courtesy of the American Numismatic Society, 1944.100.41646)

Figure 2.23. A silver coin (*denarius*) of Titus from 80 CE depicting on its obverse a portrait of Titus and his imperial titles, which continue on the reverse. The reverse depicts a curule chair surmounted by a laurel crown. (Courtesy of the American Numismatic Society, 1941.131.752)

Figure 2.24. A drain corresponding with the water channel at the upper level of the Colosseum (American Academy in Rome, Photographic Archive)

Figure 2.25. Detail of figural stuccowork in the vaults leading to the imperial box on the short axis on the northern side (Photograph: Nathan T. Elkins, 2017)

The Seating

The seating capacity of the Colosseum is another topic debated among scholars. The Chronographer of 354 CE claims that this amphitheater could accommodate 87,000 spectators, whereas the estimates of modern scholars tend to be lower, at around 50,000 to 55,000 spectators.[28] Ancient authors routinely exaggerated figures for seating capacities and participants in battle or games, and so one must always exercise caution. But we cannot make comparisons on the basis of modern sporting arenas either, for the Romans probably had a less generous definition of personal space than people in the modern, Western world. Additionally, the ancient Romans were smaller and thinner than industrialized Western populations today; the average Roman adult male was approximately 5.5 feet tall (167.6 centimeters). Rome at the time of the Colosseum's dedication was a city of a million people or more. The Colosseum could thus accommodate between approximately 5 and 9 percent of the city's population, using modern estimates at the lower end and the figure stated by the Chronographer of 354 CE at the upper end. As high as this is, it still pales in comparison with the capacity of Rome's largest entertainment building, the Circus Maximus, which could accommodate up to 150,000 spectators, according to modern estimates, or up to 250,000 spectators, approximately a quarter of the city's inhabitants, according to Pliny.[29] Entire neighborhoods would become largely vacant during the games, requiring the deployment of security forces on the streets to prevent theft and looting, in addition to providing security in entertainment venues themselves.[30]

Unlike the Circus Maximus, despised by the aristocratic authors of our ancient sources for the mixing of social classes that occurred there on account of the "first-come, first-served" allotment of seating, seats in the Colosseum and all other Roman amphitheaters and theaters were assigned according to one's social status and rank. Those who occupied the best seats nearest the arena floor were of the senatorial nobility; the equestrian class occupied the middle area, while the plebeians, the lowest class of Roman citizens, occupied the levels above the equestrians. The upper areas of the Colosseum were for freedmen, slaves, and perhaps foreign visitors, while women were further separated and sat in the absolute highest section in the *porticus* (portico) that crowned the top of the seating area (figure 2.7). It is certain that noncitizen foreigners watched the spectacles, for Martial mentions their presence among the crowd several times in his *Book of Spectacles*.[31]

Evidence for ordered seating goes back to 194 BCE when Publius Scipio Africanus, who had famously defeated Hannibal at the Battle of Zama, ending the Second Punic War, gave precedence to the senators.[32] Lucius Roscius Otho authored a law in 67 BCE that reserved the seats above the senators for the equestrians.[33] Since the equestrian class was a much larger group of citizens than the senators, seats were not guaranteed for individual members of the equestrian class as they were for the senators; there are also recorded incidences of nonequestrians infiltrating the equestrian seating area, which was probably impossible for senators due to the closer monitoring of senatorial seating.[34] Prompted by the denial of a seat for a senator at games in Puteoli, Augustus issued perhaps the most famous of all Roman laws governing seating arrangements in the latter 20s BCE, the *Lex Julia Theatralis*.[35] This law also addressed the seating of nonelite groups, including soldiers, plebeians (the lowest freeborn citizen class), and boys and their teachers, and put respectable women at the top.

When one visits the ruins of the Colosseum today, it is hard to imagine the tiers of seats rising from the podium around the arena floor to the upper levels, for time has stripped away most of the *cavea*, which rested on the inner superstructure and on the barrel vaults that formed the ambulatories and radial passages. Where the tops of vaults are still present, visitors might imagine seats on top of those (figure 2.19). *Cavea* is a Latin word that scholars use to refer to various seating areas in Roman amphitheaters and entertainment buildings, whereas *cunei* (singular: *cuneus*) are the individual wedges of seating within different parts of the *cavea*. The terms *ima cavea*, *media cavea*, and *summa cavea* refer respectively to the lowest, middle, and highest seating levels and roughly correspond with areas for equestrians, plebeians, and noncitizens and women. More-precise terms scholars use to describe the *cavea* in the Colosseum are *maenianum primum* (first gallery), *maenianum imum secundum* (lowest second gallery), *maenianum summum secundum* (highest second gallery), and the *maenianum summum in ligneis* (the highest gallery in wood).

The senators did not sit in what we call the *maenianum primum* or the *ima cavea* in the Colosseum, for they sat on the podium, immediately adjacent to, and around, the arena floor. These seats provided the best views of spectacles on the arena floor. The podium consisted of a wide platform and seven tiers of seats, perhaps added later, which were subdivided by fourteen *cunei* separated by walkways; between 250 and 500 senators or other important persons could occupy the platform.[36] Senators sat on movable wooden benches called *subsellia* (singular: *subsellium*) that were padded with cushions for comfort. The senators' attendants or slaves brought in the *subsellia* for the games, as they were not permanent fixtures on the podium. In the 1930s, during the rule of the Italian dictator Benito Mussolini, a wedge of senatorial seating on the podium was reconstructed. Unfortunately, that wedge of seating, which still lies just to the north of the eastern entrance on the long axis, is reconstructed incorrectly, having been conceived of as modern, bleacher-style seats for the senators (figure 2.19). The spots for individual senators were inscribed in stone with the names of the occupants for whom they were reserved in the fifth century CE; one might assume that they were similarly marked in the Flavian era.

Immediately above the podium and seven tiers of seats was the *maenianum primum* (what some call the *ima cavea*), which corresponded with the upper part of the first level (figure 2.7). This area was reserved for the equestrians and was subdivided into sixteen wedges of seating. The next areas, the *maenianum imum secundum* and the *maenianum summum secundum*, which together some scholars call the *media cavea*, accommodated the plebeians. These seats for the plebeians corresponded with the second level of the Colosseum. These seating areas hosted the plebeians who wore the *toga*, a mark of Roman citizenship, and the *pullus*, a darker cloak. Those wearing the *toga* sat in the lower section, the *maenianum imum secundum*, and those in the *pullus* sat in the upper part of this section, the *maenianum summum secundum*.[37] All men of means wore the clothing that denoted their social station at games in the Colosseum, for these were serious events of religious and civic significance. The plebeians with the *toga* were presumably citizens with greater financial means, since they owned the garment that marked their citizenship and that was to be worn at certain public and civic functions, as at public games. Those who wore the *pullus* were poorer. There is some evidence that by at least the second century CE, the dress code at amphitheater games became more relaxed, as citizens started to attend the games wearing attire that was more casual.

Above the *maenianum secundum*, in an area that corresponds with the upper part of the third level and beyond a tall wall, was the last set of stone seating, which hosted the lowest of Roman society: freedmen, slaves, and perhaps foreign visitors. It was in the very highest level that respectable women sat in wooden seats (in the *maenianum summum in ligneis*). This highest area was enclosed within a *porticus*, as is also visible on Flavian coins that show spectators within the amphitheater (figure 2.12) and reconstructed in the model in Rome (figure 2.2). The *porticus* would have provided shade superior to other sections of the amphitheater; thus, it would have protected the light complexion of respectable women, which was an indicator of their high status, for only a working-class woman would have had tanned skin. Without a doubt, some re-spectable women sat in other parts of the amphitheater. A section of seating on the podium, alongside the senators, was reserved for the Vestal Virgins, priestesses who guarded the sacred fire of Vesta, as were seats for other groups of priests. The empress would have sat with the emperor and his retinue in a viewing box on the podium, which would have had its own shade covering. Working plebeian women would have sat with their husbands and/or families in the appropriate seating area. Each of the seating areas in the *cavea* was sepa-rated by walls that made clear distinctions between the various social orders and classes (see the model, figure 2.2, and section drawing, figure 2.7). Seating areas were bounded by elliptical walkways. Numbered tickets corresponded with specific entrances that led to the appropriate stairways and passageways to take a spectator to his or her seating section; this would have minimized, or even prevented, the mixing of the classes.

Some groups in Rome had the privilege of reserved seats for themselves and their associates. In a famous inscription from the *Acta Fratrum Arvalium* (Acts of the Arval Brethren) dated to 81 CE, the group of twelve priests who looked after the soil's fertility reserved 92 seats in the Colosseum for persons other than themselves, as the priests would have sat on the podium.[38] They had 32 reserved seats in the area for the equestrians, 16 in the section for plebeian citi-zens, and 44 in the gallery of wooden seats at the top. The reserved seats for the equestrians and plebeians may have been for clients of the priests, while the 44 reserved wooden seats in the *porticus* were probably for the wives of the priests and the wives of the equestrians for whom the priests had reserved seats in that section.

The Imperial Viewing Box and the *Pulvinar*

An important lesson for students of Roman archaeology and history, and in-deed for anyone, is to interrogate the evidence behind statements and assump-tions that have become regarded as fact, for sometimes the evidence behind certain claims is shaky and the facts are taken for granted. An example of this is the presumed location of the emperor's box on one of the short axes on the podium of the Colosseum and the occupants of the box on the opposite side (the two boxes on the short axis are delineated at either edge of the arena in figure 2.5; in figure 2.19 both the northern [left] and southern [right] viewing boxes appear on either side of the podium at the central edges of the arena). It is apt to assume that the emperor occupied one of these boxes, because amphitheaters outside of Rome typically hosted a viewing box for the *editor* or *munerarius*, the sponsor of games, on one side of the podium on the short axis. Indeed, Suetonius tells us that, in his wooden amphitheater, the emperor Nero sat in a box on the podium so close to the spectacles that during an execution he was splattered with blood when a condemned criminal was dressed up in the guise of Icarus and pushed off a tall platform, landing very close to the emperor.[39] One will frequently read in modern literature on the Colosseum that the imperial viewing box was located on the southern side of the short axis, while the box on the opposite side was reserved for some other official or privileged person or group of people, such as the empress, the consuls, the prefect of the city, foreign envoys, certain magistrates, or the Vestal Virgins. The particularly popular assumption that the box on the opposite side was for the Vestal Virgins may derive from Suetonius's recording that Augustus reserved a space at games for the Vestal Virgins opposite the *praetor*'s tribunal.[40] Nevertheless, the Colosseum was constructed more than half a century after Augustus's death and in the city of Rome, where the emperor took precedence over the *praetor*. The Vestal Virgins could easily have had some other area reserved on the podium with the senators, as did other groups of priests.

Certainly, one of the boxes on the short axis was for the emperor. The assumption that the emperor sat on the southern side stems from statements made by the Italian archaeologist Giuseppe Lugli, whose work dates to the middle of the twentieth century. He claimed that the emperor sat in an imperial box on the short axis of the southern side of the Colosseum, since that platform could be accessed by a richly decorated subterranean passageway popularly called the Cryptoporticus of Commodus, which is often assumed to have served the function of a secret entrance for the emperor (figure 2.20).[41] According to brick stamps, the tunnel was built in the reign of Domitian, when the substructures were added, or early in the second century CE; it was given its fanciful name in the modern era, since Cassius Dio records that the emperor Commodus (180–192 CE) was attacked in a narrow entrance while entering the Colosseum.[42]

This modern projection onto the past, through a forced association with a passage in an ancient text, appears to be the basis for the assumption that the tunnel was a secret imperial entrance. The excavated course of the tunnel leads, however, in the direction of a structure near the Temple of Deified Claudius on the Caelian Hill, and it makes no sense that the emperor would have entered or exited underground to or from this direction; the emperors did not live in that part of the city. Instead, the tunnel probably served some cultic function, as the excavator suggested.[43] The tunnel may have communicated with a small building next to the temple that served the priests of the Deified Claudius. That the building was for the use of these priests is implied by inscriptions discovered in the area of that structure. The only practical reason, then, to posit the southern platform as the location of the emperor's box is the sun's glare, which would have been less of a problem on that side.[44]

Owing to the probable cultic function of the subterranean passage, the southern platform was probably instead a *pulvinar*, a viewing platform for images and attributes of the gods, goddesses, and deified emperors and their family members. This, in turn, would place the imperial box on the northern side of the short axis, where the cross erected by Mussolini now stands, and where tourists currently enter into the area around the arena (figure 2.21).[45] In theaters, images and attributes of the gods, deified emperors, and honored members of the imperial family were allotted prime seats in the *orchestra*. In the Circus Maximus, images and attributes of the same deities and individuals were brought in during a procession preceding the races and placed on the *pulvinar*. Even at the *naumachiae*, large artificial basins excavated to host large-scale mock naval battles, images seem to have been set up to watch spectacles. Cassius Dio writes that in the grove of Gaius and Lucius, where Augustus built a *naumachia*, Titus held a naval battle and kicked off the first day of spectacles in that venue by covering the lake over with a wooden platform for a gladiatorial combat and an animal hunt. He says that the wooden planks were laid out over the lake "in front of the images."[46]

The ubiquity of the presence of the images and attributes of the gods and deified emperors and their family members at the Circus Maximus, the theaters, and *naumachiae* in Rome, and also in amphitheaters and other entertainment venues outside of Rome, suggests that the Colosseum must have also had a *pulvinar*, lest it be some strange exception in the Roman world. The presence of the *pulvinar* directly across from the emperor's box can be reasonably posited by attention to the archaeology of other amphitheaters, which have a shrine on the short axis across from the *editor*'s box. For instance, at Lugdunum (modern Lyons, France), the excavators identified a shrine, perhaps dedicated to the Deified Augustus, on the short axis, and there may also be one in the same position at the amphitheater in Avenches, Switzerland. Other amphitheaters had small temples built into the *summa cavea*, as is the case with the small temple to Ephesian Diana at the amphitheater in Leptis Magna in modern Libya (Diana was often honored in amphitheaters as goddess of the hunt). In the Circus

Maximus, the arrangement of the *pulvinar* across from the finishing box, from which the emperor descended to crown victorious charioteers, offers another prototype. The subterranean passage called the Cryptoporticus of Commodus, which seems to have communicated with the building for the college of priests of the Deified Claudius next to the Temple of the Deified Claudius, would have allowed priests and attendants to transport chairs and couches that supported images and attributes. Thereby, the priests avoided the tens of thousands of spectators outside, who might impede the tasks of the priests and who might pollute the sacred objects. Divine images and attributes, paraded at the games to their place on the *pulvinar*, were often stored in the buildings of priestly colleges when not in use, according to ancient texts and inscriptions.

The platforms on the northern and southern axes of the Colosseum are quite large (12 meters [39.4 feet] wide). The imperial box would have comfortably accommodated the emperor, empress, and their family, along with attendants, advisers, honored guests of the emperor, and some of his personal bodyguard. The imperial box could have held up to 60 people, while the *pulvinar* on the southern side would have seated images and attributes for Rome's most important gods, goddesses, the deified emperors and empresses, and other members of the imperial family who had been voted honorary chairs at games.[47] Indeed, coins of Titus and early in Domitian's reign, which are contemporary with the inauguration of the Colosseum and the earliest games there, depict draped seats that support the attributes of Jupiter (a winged thunderbolt) (figure 2.22), Minerva (a Corinthian helmet), and supporting semicircular and triangular *struppi* (archaizing images or attributes made from twigs and vines) that generically symbolized past deified emperors and empresses. Other coins show a curule chair supporting a laurel crown (figure 2.23), which perhaps denoted the presence of the living emperor whether he was present or not. The Senate voted Julius Caesar the honor of a chair and crown placed among the gods in the *orchestra* of theaters during his lifetime. Coins of Octavian, who became known as Augustus in 27 BCE, depict Caesar's chair surmounted by a laurel crown, which is identical to the representation on Titus's coins, except that on Octavian's coins the chair is inscribed with Caesar's name and his title of *dictator*. Additional coins of Titus and Domitian depict a dolphin coiled around an anchor that symbolized Neptune, a dolphin on a tripod that symbolized Apollo, and a lighted altar that symbolized Vesta. Coins of this series were misunderstood for most of the twentieth century as having depicted *pulvinaria* set up around Rome to appease the gods in the aftermath of the eruption of Mount Vesuvius in 79 CE, which destroyed Pompeii and Herculaneum, and a fire in 80 CE that damaged a significant portion of the city of Rome, or as representations of the attributes and chairs set up in Rome's theaters. Their association with the dedication of the Colosseum is, however, far more probable on account of the significance of that event.[48]

The Arena Floor and the *Hypogeum*

Processions, animal fights and hunts, executions, and gladiatorial combats all took place on the Colosseum's arena floor in the center of the amphitheater. As with the amphitheater itself, the arena and the substructures below are elliptical in shape. On the long axis, the arena is just over 79 meters long (259 feet) and on the short axis it measures just over 47 meters (154 feet). When the Colosseum was first constructed and dedicated, it had no substructures. Its wooden floor sat directly on the ground and foundations until the substructures were added later in Domitian's reign, at which time the wooden floor was supported by the brick walls and piers of the substructures below. The arena floor was constructed of wooden planks and covered in sand, which absorbed the blood of animals, executed criminals and prisoners of war, and gladiators.[49] It can be hard to visualize the arena floor when one today sees nothing but the exposed tunnels and piers of the substructures below; helpfully, the arena floor has been partially reconstructed in modern times to give a sense of how the wooden floor rested upon the substructures (figure 2.19). The tall wall of the podium, upon which the senators and other important persons sat, separated the spectators from the dangerous spectacles on the arena below. At the edge of the top of the podium wall was a walkway around the arena floor; spectators may have used it, but security forces, such as the Praetorian Guard, probably also patrolled it to deal swiftly with any rogue animal or the unlikely attempt of a gladiator or condemned criminal to escape the arena floor. Protection of the high-class citizens seated near the action was essential. Animals, gladiators, and condemned criminals would have entered the arena through either the western or eastern entrances on the long axis, which led directly to the arena floor; after the completion of the substructures, they also could have entered more dramatically by means of elevators and trapdoors from below. Animals such as bulls, bears, elephants, rhinoceroses, and hippopotami were, however, too large to have been placed in cages below the arena and always would have been introduced to the arena at ground level.

The substructures below the arena floor are often called the *hypogeum* (figures 2.19–2.20). The floor of the *hypogeum* lies approximately 6.5 meters (21.3 feet) below the arena floor. Archaeologists have long had a general sense of how the substructures worked as an area in which slaves and attendants powered elevators and trapdoors, so that animals and gladiators could appear quickly and theatrically on the arena floor above. Elevators were also employed to erect and remove stage scenery and props that increased the drama of events, especially animal hunts and executions, which were made more interesting through elaborate stages, such as artificial mounds and jungles for hunts. There is evidence that, during the inaugural games, Titus flooded the arena for a small-scale naval battle (see chapter 4); after Domitian added the substructures, aquatic spectacles in the Colosseum would have been impossible. The substructures underwent many changes and renovations over the centuries after they were first constructed.[50]

Around the perimeter of the substructures are 32 bays that probably functioned as stalls for animals that were to appear in the shows. There is a central tunnel on the long axis of the *hypogeum*, flanked by two parallel corridors; around these are three curved corridors, echoing the shape of the arena itself. Astute observers may see cuttings on the sides of the walls of the substructures that accommodated the wooden beams and equipment for the various elevators and trapdoors. In some places, circular fittings in the floor of the substructures are visible. These held capstans that raised and lowered the elevators and cages. Substructures were common amenities in amphitheaters in Italy and in the Roman provinces.

Beneath the eastern and western ends on the long axis are also tunnels with bays and large open rooms, the purposes of which are unknown (figure 2.20). Perhaps gladiators mustered here or condemned criminals contemplated their deaths just before the games; or perhaps the rooms contained stage equipment and props for the spectacles. The tunnel on the eastern end of the long axis connected the Colosseum's *hypogeum* with the Ludus Magnus, a gladiator school just to the east of the amphitheater, the remains of which are still visible today. Gladiators could thus move directly from their barracks to the Colosseum and appear on the arena above by means of an elevator. On the floors of the tunnels is also evidence of winches, which probably pulled heavy stage equipment into the *hypogeum* from storage, so that it could be lifted to the arena floor above; this would suggest that at least some of the rooms beneath the eastern and western sides of the amphitheater were used for storing stage equipment and scenery.

Drains, Fountains, and Toilets

As one might expect, there is an elaborate and sophisticated system of drains that empty into sewers below the Colosseum. The Colosseum is, after all, in essence a giant bowl that would collect rainwater, and so drainage was key. In addition to the disposal of rainwater, drains were essential because the Colosseum also had drinking fountains and toilets for the comfort of the spectators. Excavations of the drains have provided evidence that spectators snacked in the amphitheater on meat and nuts, just as modern spectators might at a baseball, football, or soccer stadium.

Astute visitors will still see evidence for ancient drains (figure 2.24) and fountains throughout the amphitheater today.[51] One may see remnants of fountains either through square-shaped recesses in the floor with a channel for a drainpipe to direct the water flow into a base or through cross-shaped cuttings in the wall that held pipes that fed a figural fountain spout. On the first level alone, eleven fountains have been identified along with another seventeen possible fountains. They are located on piers between the second and third annular passageways and next to stairs that ascend to the second level. Another sixteen fountains may have been located on the side of the third passageway that was next to stairs that led to the podium. Additional evidence for fountains is found in the upper levels, where pipes run between the levels. Although the Colosseum was the largest and most sophisticated of all Roman amphitheaters, it was not alone in its possession of a system of drains, fountains, and toilets; Puteoli, for instance, also had an extensive water system to drain its amphitheater.

Spectators in Roman amphitheaters and theaters were often sprayed with saffron-scented water, which might be done by pipes and mechanisms installed in the *cavea* but more probably by attendants passing through the seating areas.[52] Literary evidence suggests that this golden, saffron spray was probably restricted to those in senatorial sections, for the manufacture of such a spray was very expensive and its distribution was an ostentatious display of wealth and extravagance. Attendants may also have sprayed the mucked arena with saffron to mask the smell of death and blood. That spectators in the Colosseum also were sprinkled with saffron is implied by Martial who says "here [in the amphitheater] the Cilicians have been sprayed with their own mist," for Cilicia was an important source for saffron.[53]

Decoration

The Colosseum today is a ruin of broken stones and brick-faced concrete walls. It is hard to imagine that the building was, in fact, richly decorated millennia ago. As discussed previously, the arcades on the façade of the second and third levels contained statues and sculpture groups, which in total would have numbered 160, including the *quadrigae* that sat above the elaborated entrances on the axes, and bronze shields were placed between the large windows of the highest level. We often conceive of the Colosseum as a white, stone building and the statues that were originally in its arcades as white marble; indeed, this is what reconstruction drawings and models show us. Thanks to numerous studies over the past several decades, we now know that virtually all marble sculptures, whether freestanding or in relief, were brightly painted in Greek and Roman antiquity. Colors such as red, blue, and yellow prevailed. Even the flesh of the subjects was covered in paint, as nothing was left bare. For the Greeks and Romans, white marble was simply a blank canvas to receive color. They also painted architectural elements; those gleaming white marble temples we are accustomed to imagining were, in fact, garishly painted. We must, therefore, accept that the statuary in the Colosseum's façade and probably parts of the façade itself (e.g., the columns and pilasters) were painted in a similar fashion. The paint would have increased the legibility of sculptural subjects, especially those at higher levels.

The interiors of Roman amphitheaters also bore rich decoration. A veneer of various colored marbles could be placed in different parts of the amphitheater, as was the case in the Colosseum. The high walls between the various parts of the *cavea* that separated social classes from one another would have been elaborated with marble panels and statues. Sculptural and architectural fragments abound in the Colosseum: column capitals, bases, and drums, broken figures, and balustrades.[54] The *porticus* in the *summa cavea*, where respectable women sat, was supported by Corinthian columns and probably also hosted imported marbles of various colors and large-scale statues. At the amphitheater at Capua, balustrades on the *vomitoria* (singular: *vomitorium*), entrances and exits that opened on the *cavea*, were encrusted with marble decoration. Fragments of some balustrades in the forms of hunting dogs catching their prey have been found there; there is also a relief of the goddess Diana performing a hunt. The Colosseum's balustrades were also decorated sumptuously with marble sculptures around the *vomitoria* that opened into the *cavea* and onto a spread of marble walkways and rows of seats. Some balustrade fragments in the

Colosseum, dated to the third or fourth century CE, which may echo the subjects from earlier periods, show hunting dogs and their prey, winged griffins, and *cornucopiae*, among other subjects. These too would have been painted.

Plaster adorned the vaults of the ambulatories, and remnants of white plaster are still visible in various parts of the Colosseum. These plastered areas come from the latest phases of the Colosseum. Excavations of the drains and sewers below the Colosseum have yielded plaster fragments of yellow, green, red, and black, suggesting that in earlier phases, including when the Colosseum was first dedicated under Titus, walls and vaults were covered in bright colors and perhaps also were decorated with figural scenes. Glass and golden *tesserae* (the individual pieces that form a mosaic) have also been found, suggesting that the Colosseum was home to extraordinary mosaics. Figural stuccowork was another medium of decoration, especially in the vaults of Roman amphitheaters. The Flavian amphitheater at Puteoli contains some well-preserved stucco decoration. Thousands of visitors to the Colosseum today, failing to look up, miss the remarkably well-preserved stucco decoration that survives in the Colosseum. In the vault of the northern axial entrance that leads to the emperor's box is a section of stucco molded into relief and bearing figural scenes (figure 2.25).[55] These were extensively studied, drawn, and recorded during the Renaissance, when they were better preserved. Similar stuccos probably also decorated the vaults leading to the *pulvinar* on the opposite side of the podium.

The Colosseum was the king of amphitheaters in the Roman world and a paragon of Roman engineering prowess. The realization of the building was a testament to the power of the Roman emperor and the resources of the Roman people. It took an army of people to construct the amphitheater and another army to maintain the building and to care for its amenities during the games, such as the substructures, the awning, and the water system. Except for the radically different sorts of entertainments offered then, the Colosseum was a remarkably modern building in the sense of the spectators' experience as they were led by numbered tickets that directed them to the appropriate entryways, passageways and stairs, and seating sections; additionally, a spectator could get up to visit lavatories and fountains, and perhaps even to purchase snacks during the long day of spectacles. Although the Colosseum was the biggest and most elaborate of the Flavian building projects, it was but one component of the Flavian building program, lying at the heart of a complex of buildings that together communicated the idea of Flavian dynastic legitimacy and hegemony.

-III-

An Amphitheater in the Heart of Rome

AS A BUILDING FOR mass entertainment, an amphitheater the size of the Colosseum was an extravagant gift to the urban population of Rome. At the time of its dedication in 80 CE, it filled an apparent need for a large-scale permanent venue for gladiatorial combats and associated arena spectacles in the city of Rome. Statilius Taurus, one of Octavian's generals, had built the first stone amphitheater in Rome in 30 BCE.[1] Caligula is said to have begun work on an amphitheater next to the Saepta Julia, a building in the Campus Martius where people assembled to vote but also where gladiatorial games were sometimes held; it is unclear whether Caligula's amphitheater was a wooden or stone construction, but it was never fully realized. Nero built a wooden amphitheater in 57 CE.[2] Both the Amphitheater of Statilius Taurus and Nero's wooden amphitheater were destroyed in the Great Fire of 64 CE. Rome was thus without a proper venue for gladiators and arena spectacles for sixteen years, until the Colosseum's inauguration.

Indeed, the Colosseum is sometimes cynically viewed in the context of "bread and circuses," as an imperial diversion and propaganda to placate the masses. Such a view is sorely incomplete and simplistic. To understand the political and dynastic significance of the Colosseum, one must remember the events of Nero's fall and Vespasian's rise to power and be conversant with other parts of Vespasian's building program, as these inform how the Colosseum and other Flavian monuments communicated Flavian legitimacy and dynastic aspirations.

The Flavian Building Program

When Vespasian came to power, he embarked upon a building program centered on the area of Nero's Domus Aurea.[3] He would thus transform Rome and simultaneously erode Nero's mark on the city (compare the plan of Nero's Domus Aurea, figure 1.6, with the plan of Flavian building in this area, figure 3.1).

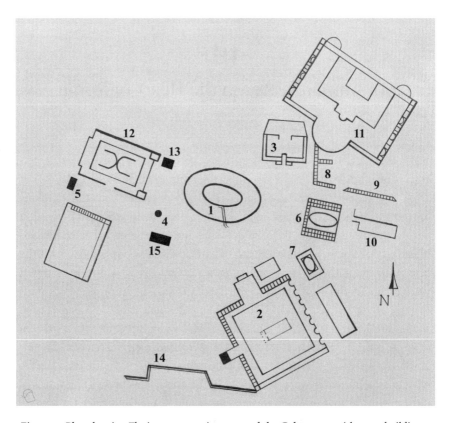

Figure 3.1. Plan showing Flavian constructions around the Colosseum, with some buildings from other periods for reference: 1. The Colosseum, indicated with the Cryptoporticus of Commodus; 2. The Temple of the Deified Claudius; 3. The Baths of Titus; 4. The Meta Sudans; 5. The Arch of Titus; 6. The Ludus Magnus; 7. The Ludus Matutinus (?); 8. The Ludus Dacicus; 9. The Castra Misenatum; 10. The Armamentarium (?). Earlier and later buildings: 11. The Baths of Trajan, completed in the reign of Trajan (98-117 CE); 12. The Temple of Venus and Roma, completed in circa 135 CE; 13. The Colossus of Sol, formerly the Colossus of Nero, moved to this location in circa 128 CE; 14. The Aqua Claudia, completed in the reign of Claudius (41-54 CE); 15. The Arch of Constantine, dedicated in circa 315 CE. Note: The Temple of Peace does not appear on this plan but lies to the west of the Temple of Venus and Roma (12) and among the imperial *fora*. (Drawing: Cade Kegerreis)

In addition to the amphitheater, which he built on Nero's '
pleted the Temple of the Deified Claudius and the Temp'
work on other structures in the area. When Titus inaugurate.
he also dedicated his baths, on which construction must have a.
during Vespasian's reign. Domitian completed a fountain known as th.
Sudans and a triumphal arch dedicated to the Deified Titus, and he built fo.
gladiator schools. Together, these monuments communicated a uniquely Flavian political ideology, which promoted the Flavians' legitimacy not only by
celebrating their victories in Judaea but also by portraying them as worthy successors of the Deified Augustus and the Deified Claudius.

The Temple of the Deified Claudius

The Temple of the Deified Claudius occupied a prominent position on the
top of the Caelian Hill, immediately to the southeast of the Colosseum.[4] The
scale of the temple complex was quite large. The area it covered is greater than
that of the Colosseum, for its terrace occupies a space of 200 meters (656 feet)
by 180 meters (590.5 feet). Construction on the temple began after Claudius's
death, early in the reign of Nero, at the behest of Agrippina. After the murder
of his mother, Nero allowed work on the temple to halt. Still visible along the
Via Claudia is the eastern buttress wall of the temple terrace, which Nero had
transformed into a *nymphaeum* to feed his great lake (figure 3.2; this is the scal-
loped wall indicated on figure 3.1). Parts of the temple platform survive in rus-
ticated travertine blocks, now incorporated into the Basilica of Saints John and
Paul on the Caelian Hill; nothing survives of the temple itself. The use of rusti-
cated blocks in the construction of the temple platform was an homage to
Claudius, for he seems to have been fond of the style, as it was widely deployed
in his reign; Claudius's archaizing interests, which included the Etruscans, may
have been the source for the popularity of that style of construction during his
rule. A grand staircase on the northern side of the temple descended in the direction of the Colosseum's southern façade. Completion of the temple portrayed Vespasian as a dutiful steward of Rome who piously attended to the
memories of "good" emperors of the past, such as the Deified Claudius, while
snubbing Nero's memory.

Figure 3.2. The eastern terrace wall of the Temple of the Deified Claudius, transformed by Nero into a *nymphaeum*, located on the Via Claudia (Photograph: Nathan T. Elkins, 2017)

The Temple of Peace

Another temple complex that Vespasian completed was the Temple of Peace, often referred to as the Forum of Peace.[5] The Temple of Peace is a short walk from the Colosseum; it lies to its west, beyond the Temple of Venus and Roma that Hadrian completed in circa 135 CE, and the Basilica of Maxentius and Constantine that Constantine finished in circa 312 CE. It is next to the Forum of Augustus and is often conceived of as a third imperial forum (Julius Caesar's was the first). Vespasian dedicated the Temple of Peace in 75 CE. In the Roman world, peace was not thought of as the opposite of war, as it is today, but instead as the outcome of war and victory. The Temple of Peace was thus an ideologically charged monument, dedicated to the goddess Peace (Pax) in the aftermath of the Flavian victories in Judaea and the conclusion of the Jewish Revolt with the capture of Jerusalem in 71 CE. A Flavian monument to peace carried strong ideological associations with the Deified Augustus, for Augustus had instituted a long period of peace after the successful conclusion of various wars and closed the doors of the Temple of Janus three times during his reign (at times of peace the doors of this temple were closed, whereas when Rome was at war they were opened). In 13 BCE, the Senate voted to honor Augustus's return to Rome with the construction of the monumental Altar of Peace (Ara Pacis), which was completed in 9 BCE. In Vespasian's Temple of Peace, Greek artworks were on display, as were spoils taken from the Temple in Jerusalem. Domitian began constructing an imperial forum with a temple to his tutelary goddess, Minerva, between the Temple of Peace and the Forum of Augustus later in his reign; he was assassinated before its completion, and so the emperor Nerva (96–98 CE) dedicated it as the Forum of Nerva.

The Baths of Titus

Titus dedicated his public baths at the same time as the Colosseum in 80 CE.[6] The Baths of Titus lie just to the northeast of the Colosseum on the southern edge of the Oppian Hill and were built over parts of Nero's Domus Aurea. Later, Trajan (98–117 CE) built another set of baths immediately to the northeast of Titus's baths. The only extant remnants of the Baths of Titus that one may see in Rome today are piers of the *porticus* (figure 3.3), which are across the street from the Colosseum's northern façade and near the entrance to the Colosseo metro station. The *porticus* of the Baths of Titus appears not only on

Figure 3.3. Piers of the *porticus* of the Baths of Titus to the northeast of the Colosseum (Photograph: Nathan T. Elkins, 2017)

coins of Titus and Domitian (figure 2.12) but also behind and slightly to the right of the Colosseum in the digital model showing the amphitheater and surrounding buildings from the vantage point of the terrace of the Temple of the Deified Claudius (figure 2.3).

Titus's baths were, like the Colosseum, a generous gift to the people. In ancient Rome, public baths were subsidized and thus very accessible. Most Romans bathed regularly. Public bath complexes were centers for gathering and social interactions; they included lecture halls, libraries, gardens, open courtyards for athletic exercise, and sweat rooms, as well as hot baths (a *caldarium*), warm baths (a *tepidarium*), cold baths (a *frigidarium*), and a swimming pool (*natatio*). To heat the baths, the lead floor of a bath was suspended over columns of bricks, which archaeologists call a hypocaust system; slaves constantly stoked furnaces so that heated air would be pumped into the hypocaust system to warm the waters. Titus often bathed in his public baths, alongside the common people.[7]

The Meta Sudans

Another significant monument near the Colosseum, which Domitian completed, is the Meta Sudans, a large conical fountain just to the southwest of the amphitheater (see figure 2.3).[8] The concrete core of the Meta Sudans was still visible until 1936 when Mussolini had it and the base of the Colossus of Sol removed because they were unattractive and because he wished to orchestrate parades of soldiers through the Arch of Constantine to the Via dell'Impero, the modern road he built that wraps around the Colosseum (figure 3.4). Before Mussolini's removal of the concrete core of the superstructure of the Meta Sudans, it stood approximately 8 meters (26.25 feet) tall, and the fountain was originally double that height in antiquity. Today, the site of the Meta Sudans is outlined in stone just to the north of the present location of the Arch of Constantine. The Chronographer of 354 CE attributes the Meta Sudans to Domitian's reign, although the provisional fountain appeared next to the Colosseum on coins of Titus in 80 CE, a design replicated on the coins of Domitian for the Deified Titus in circa 81/82 CE (figure 2.12). Study of the masonry and the discovery of a brick stamp prove a Domitianic date, as do recent excavations in the area that suggest the Meta Sudans was constructed during a single building phase when work on the Colosseum was well underway. It is probable then that it was either Vespasian's or Titus's vision to construct the fountain, that work began during Titus's short reign, and that it was left to Domitian to finish the

Figure 3.4. A photograph from the 1890s of the exposed core of the Meta Sudans, to the southwest of the Colosseum and immediately north of the Arch of Constantine (Everett Historical/Shutterstock)

project. The "Sweating Turning Post," which is how "Meta Sudans" translates, is so named because the conical shape is that of a turning post (*meta*) in the Circus Maximus and water trickled down from the top of it into a basin.

The Meta Sudans had strong ideological associations with the Deified Augustus; beneath the Meta Sudans, excavations recently have revealed a fountain of similar shape that was erected during the reign of Augustus. Augustus divided Rome into fourteen administrative regions, and four of them joined at the crossroads marked by his Meta Sudans and later by the Flavian Meta Sudans. There is additional significance for the Augustan Meta Sudans: nearby was one of the four corners of the sacred boundary (*pomerium*) of the city of Rome, plowed in 753 BCE by Romulus, the legendary founder and first king of Rome. Augustus was also born in a neighborhood near to this spot. For Augustus, the monument drew strong parallels between the lives and actions of Romulus and Augustus, who was widely portrayed in art and contemporary literature as a second founder of Rome. Brenda Longfellow has intensively studied the ideological significance of both the Augustan and the Flavian Meta Sudans in terms of their form and location. The conical shape of the fountains is similar to that of a *baetulus* (anglicized as "baetyl"), an aniconic stone that served the function of a cult statue or cult symbol of a god. A similar *baetulus* appears in numerous instances in Augustan art associated with the worship of Apollo, Augustus's tutelary deity. The Temple of Apollo stood nearby on the Palatine Hill, and Apollo was also the god credited with Octavian's victory over Antony and Cleopatra at the Battle of Actium in 31 BCE, which precipitated his annexation of Egypt. Two *baetuli* have been recovered in excavations at the Greek city of Nikopolis (literally "City of Victory"), a city that Octavian later founded at the site of his headquarters immediately prior to the Battle of Actium.

The Augustan fountain and the intersection of the roads where it was located were transformed under Nero after the Great Fire of 64 CE, when he began construction on his Domus Aurea in this area. After Nero's death, the Flavian emperors restored the roadways here to their Augustan pattern. Their building of an enlarged Meta Sudans on this spot firmly and piously linked them, and their reorganization of Rome, with the Deified Augustus and his own reorganization of the city, while simultaneously contrasting their rule with Nero, who disrupted Augustan urban planning. Vespasian was, in a way, a third founder of Rome, and this monument presented him and the Flavians as such. There were certainly many people in Rome who would have remembered Augustus's fountain and the topography of the surrounding area prior to the Great Fire of 64 CE and Nero's Domus Aurea at the time when the Flavians were making this bold visual link by building their own Meta Sudans.

The Arch of Titus

The Arch of Titus was dedicated by the Senate and Roman People to the Deified Titus early in the reign of Domitian, although it is quite possible that work began in Titus's reign.[9] It stands astride the ancient road known as the Sacra Via (Sacred Way) as one enters the Forum Romanum from the direction of the Colosseum valley. Since the time of the Republic, Roman generals could be voted the honor of a triumph for conquests and victories in foreign wars.[10] The triumph consisted of a procession through the city on a prescribed route that terminated at the Temple of Jupiter Optimus Maximus on the Capitoline Hill. In the parade, the triumphing general rode in a tall chariot in garb resembling the god Jupiter himself, while his soldiers marched in the procession with him. Also in the parade were prisoners of war and spoils from the enemy and conquered lands. Carried in the procession were signs that identified what the spoils consisted of and their significance and paintings that showed important battles and events during the military campaigns. Under the emperors, the honor of a triumph was reserved exclusively for the emperor and members of the imperial family. Oftentimes a triumphal arch would be erected on the route of the procession sometime after the emperor celebrated his triumph in Rome. The arch stood as a permanent reminder of the emperor's victory, and all future triumphing emperors would process through it during their own triumphs.

Vespasian and Titus celebrated a triumph together for the successful conclusion of the Jewish Revolt in 71 CE, after Titus captured Jerusalem and returned to Rome to join his father. The Arch of Titus honors, however, only Titus. At the apex of the underside of the arch is an image of Titus on the back of an eagle, symbolizing his apotheosis. On the interior of the northern pier, a relief depicts Titus riding in his triumphal *quadriga*, holding a palm branch and Jupiter's scepter. It is not a literal rendition of the triumph, for the goddess Victory stands behind him in his chariot and crowns him with a laurel wreath; escorting the chariot is the *genius* (spirit) of the Roman People and the *genius* of the Senate. The personification of Roma, the goddess of the city herself, leads the chariot. In front of and alongside the chariot are *lictores*, bodyguards who were assigned to certain Roman magistrates. These *lictores* are depicted holding a bundle of rods bound around an axe (*fasces*), which symbolized the magistrate's power. On the interior of the southern pier is a relief that depicts spoils from the Temple in Jerusalem, sacked and destroyed by Titus's army after it breached the city's walls (figure 3.5). Men carrying a stretcher hold aloft the seven-branched menorah—wrought of solid gold—that was inside the Temple and described in the Hebrew Bible. On either side of the menorah are signs that would have described the significance of the object, and perhaps its value, to the spectators of the triumphal procession. At the right end of this panel, the procession is passing through a triumphal arch; the group of men there hold a stretcher that supports what may be the table of showbread, also of solid gold, from the Temple. The two trumpets carried by different attendants are probably the two silver trumpets that announced sacrifice at the Temple. These same spoils would have been displayed later in Vespasian's Temple of Peace.

The Gladiator Schools, Other Support Buildings, and the Castra Misenatum

According to the Chronographer of 354 CE, Domitian built four gladiatorial schools to support the games at the Colosseum. The names and general locations

Figure 3.5. Detail of the southern panel on the interior of the Arch of Titus showing the triumphal procession with men carrying spoils from the Temple in Jerusalem (Photograph: Nathan T. Elkins, 2017)

for those gladiator schools come from the *Regionaries*, a fourth-century CE document concerning the fourteen regions of Rome. The names of the four gladiator schools are the Ludus Dacicus (the Dacian School), the Ludus Gallicus (the Gallic School), the Ludus Magnus (the Great School), and the Ludus Matutinus (the Morning School) (three of these are indicated on figure 3.1).[11] The more precise locations of these gladiator schools are identifiable from fragments of the third-century CE marble plan of Rome and from inscriptions found in the areas of the buildings. In Latin, the name for a gladiator school is a *ludus*, which must not be confused with the word for public games themselves, *ludi*, which always appears in the plural form. A *ludus* was a place where gladiators trained and were lodged. Gladiator schools often specialized in producing different types of fighters. Outside of Rome, gladiator schools were typically owned and operated by a *lanista*, who oversaw the training and care of the gladiators therein. The *lanista* was often himself a former gladiator who had won or bought his freedom. In Rome, these gladiator schools were owned by the emperor and managed by officials appointed by the emperor.[12]

Domitian's construction of the gladiator schools did not have the same ideological significance as other projects previously discussed that connected the Flavians with past emperors. Instead, these were practical, as they provided direct imperial access to a diverse group of highly trained gladiators in Rome who could perform in the arena of the Colosseum. To hold gladiatorial shows, the sponsor of the games would typically rent gladiators from a *lanista* and negotiate a contract, which would include a provision for an exponentially increased rate of pay to the *lanista* if a gladiator were killed. Renting gladiators for shows was already a very expensive prospect for local magistrates in view of the risk entailed and the amount of resources a *lanista* had invested in the training, upkeep, and care of gladiators; however, the *editor* or *munerarius* could potentially put himself in grave debt if several gladiators were killed during the exhibition. In 65 BCE, Julius Caesar bought a *ludus* so that he would not have to worry about renting out gladiators for his own shows and incurring unplanned expenses upon the death of one or more gladiators. Domitian's construction and founding of state-owned gladiator schools near the Colosseum were thus quite pragmatic from a financial point of view.

The largest of Domitian's gladiator schools was the Ludus Magnus, less than half of which has been excavated. Today, one can still view its excavated remains across the street to the east of the Colosseum (figure 3.6). Walls that formed rooms around a small-scale amphitheater in which the gladiators trained are visible. The small arena measures 63 meters (206.7 feet) by 42 meters (137.8 feet). A subterranean tunnel linked the Colosseum with the Ludus Magnus, so that gladiators could be transferred securely between the two buildings. Nearby were the Ludus Dacicus, perhaps built to house and train prisoners of war from Domitian's and Trajan's campaigns in Dacia (in the area of modern Romania), and the Ludus Matutinus. Because the latter's Latin name translates to "Morning School," hunters and beast fighters were probably trained here, since wild beast hunts took place in the morning (one-on-one gladiatorial combats took place in the afternoon). The name of the Ludus Gallicus suggests it trained gladiators who fought in the Gallic style; it does not have the same level of topographical evidence as the rest, but it must have been in the same area as the others, perhaps nearer the Temple of the Deified Claudius.

Four other supporting structures merit brief comment: the Armamentarium, the Spoliarium, the Saniarium, and the Summum Choragium.[13] Although we do not know exactly when they were constructed, it is logical that they would have been built at or around the same time as Domitian constructed the four gladiator schools. The Armamentarium was an armory where weapons

Figure 3.6. The excavated remains of the Ludus Magnus, viewed from the northeast. The small rooms provided housing for gladiators; the curved wall that is partly covered by the road below the modern buildings is the outer wall of the small amphitheater in which gladiators trained. At the top right, in the background, are the arcades of the Colosseum. (Photograph: Nathan T. Elkins, 2003)

and armor for the gladiators were stored, as the *Regionaries* attests, and a fragment of the Forma Urbis Romae suggests that it was near Domitian's gladiator schools. The Spoliarium, also listed in the *Regionaries*, functioned as the place where gladiators put on their armor and equipped themselves before combat and also where the bodies of dead gladiators were stored prior to permanent disposal. If a gladiator fought in a particularly dishonorable or cowardly manner, his execution could be ordered to take place privately in the Spoliarium instead of honorably and nobly on the arena floor. Also attested by the *Regionaries* is the Sanarium, a place where wounded or sick gladiators would be taken for medical care and treatment. It must have also been near the gladiator schools and near the Armamentarium and Spoliarium. The final supporting structure listed by the *Regionaries* is the Summum Choragium, a building for the storage of large equipment and scenery used in the Colosseum's spectacles; it too was located east of the Colosseum and near the Ludus Magnus.

The Castra Misenatum was a camp in Rome where marines from the imperial fleet, headquartered at Misenum, were stationed to oversee the awnings and riggings at the Colosseum and other entertainment buildings in the capital.[14] As sailors, these men were naturally adept at manning the masts, linens, and ropes that were deployed in these complex systems. The Castra Misenatum is listed in the *Regionaries* and is also known from a fragment of the Forma Urbis Romae; its location seems to be on the northern side of the Ludus Magnus and perhaps also to its east. We do not know when the barracks for the marines was built, but it would be logical to assign its origins in the reign of Titus or Domitian, when work on the Colosseum was approaching its end phase or when the gladiator schools were installed.

The Flavians and the Julio-Claudian Connection

The Flavian building program had as one of its primary aims the erasure of Nero's repurposing of this area of the city after the Great Fire of 64 CE. Several Flavian monuments also made overt links with two deified emperors from the previous dynasty, the Deified Augustus and the Deified Claudius. When Vespasian came to power after the civil wars of 68–69 CE, he was in a unique position. None of the contenders after Nero's death had been able to maintain a hold on imperial power, but Vespasian was victorious. He had to establish a dynasty, and his regime had to project legitimacy, even though he and his family were not descended from the Julio-Claudian dynasty that Augustus founded a century before Nero's actions led to its swift extinction. The Flavian emperors and the supporters of the regime promoted ideological associations with the "good" emperors of that former dynasty to signal stability and continuity, while conspicuously overlooking the "bad" Julio-Claudians, specifically Caligula and Nero.[15] This seems to have been on the agenda from the very beginning of Vespasian's accession, for, in *Lex de Imperio Vespasiani*, the Senate conferred Augustan power upon him by invoking the names of two of Augustus's Julio-Claudian successors, Tiberius and Claudius, as precedents.[16] It was also a necessity of which the Roman public was aware, as implied by Suetonius's remark in the early second century CE that "Vespasian as yet lacked prestige and a certain divinity, so to speak, since he was an unexpected and still new made emperor."[17]

Associations with Claudius to legitimize Vespasian were sensible, as Claudius was the last of the "good" Julio-Claudian emperors before Nero. Claudius, similar to Vespasian after the civil wars, was a stabilizing force for Rome after the chaotic reign of Caligula. Vespasian's policies mirrored Claudius's in his concern for popular welfare, and he improved Claudian legislation. He even resumed military operations in Britain, a province added by Claudius; during Claudius's reign, Vespasian had served as a general in the British campaigns. Titus also promoted the commemoration of Claudius. Titus was a boyhood friend of Claudius's natural-born son, Britannicus. When he became emperor, Titus ordered a golden statue of Britannicus erected in the palace and an ivory statue of him to be brought in during processions in the Circus Maximus, which he personally attended to on its first appearance.[18] This action was an assault on Nero's memory, for Nero had supplanted Britannicus and poisoned him; Titus's command to set up the statues promoted his own associations with Claudius and his house.

The actions of Vespasian and Titus that linked them with Claudius are in line with what we see in their building programs. For instance, their restoration of Claudian aqueducts, which Nero diverted to the Domus Aurea, presented them as restorers of Rome to its pre-Neronian, Augustan, and Claudian state and as concerned for public needs. Their building program had a Claudian slant in its focus on infrastructure and public building for popular benefit. Vespasian's completion of the Temple of Deified Claudius elevated the memory of Claudius and raised him as a model for Flavian rule, in contrast with Nero. The parallels between Claudius and Vespasian were, indeed, so pronounced that if Vespasian were considered a second Claudius, then Titus might have been feared by the Roman people to become a second Nero, as Suetonius suggests.[19]

Nonetheless, Titus, far from turning into another Nero, was well remembered and duly deified upon his death in 81 CE. The Colosseum coins of Titus and Domitian for the Deified Titus illustrate a further ideological link with Claudius (figure 2.12). The reverses of the coins depict Titus seated on a curule chair holding a branch, symbolizing victory, and surrounded by arms captured in the Jewish Revolt. The only iconographic prototypes for this representation are coins of Claudius from circa 41 to 50 CE that show him in the same manner, seated on a curule chair and holding a branch, among the arms taken during his conquest of Britain (figure 3.7). These coins of Claudius would have still been in circulation, and viewers would have easily understood the similarities between the two images, as the military distinction of Titus and Claudius was compared. The obverses of the Flavian Colosseum coins depicted Flavian gifts to the people: the Colosseum, financed by the spoils from the war in Judaea, as well as the Meta Sudans and the Baths of Titus. The depiction of such structures invited comparisons with Claudius because his building program also

Figure 3.7. A bronze coin (*sestertius*) of Claudius from circa 41–54 CE, depicting on its obverse a portrait of Drusus, the father of Claudius (the hair has been reworked in modern times). The reverse depicts Claudius, seated on a curule chair, holding a branch and surrounded by captured arms from his conquest of Britain. (Formerly in the A. Bougon Coll., Clement Platt Auction [Paris], Nov. 18–19, 1935, no. 202; Photograph: Bob Smith)

focused on public benefit and welfare. A further link with Claudius may be discerned in the vantage point from which the Colosseum and the flanking monuments are depicted. Although there are variant coins that depict the Colosseum with the Meta Sudans and the *porticus* of the Baths of Titus on opposite sides, and others that omit them entirely, most surviving specimens show the Colosseum with the *porticus* on the right and Meta Sudans on the left; this is also the only variant produced under Domitian.[20] Such a view can only be achieved from a vantage point on the terrace of the Temple of the Deified Claudius (see figure 2.3). Indeed, Martial's second epigram in the *Book of Spectacles* celebrates the construction of specific Flavian monuments in the Colosseum valley on what was Nero's Domus Aurea and also mentions the Claudian *porticus* that spreads shade there; it is remarkably similar to what we see on the obverses of the Flavian Colosseum coins (the passage is quoted in chapter 1).

In addition to Claudius, the Flavians associated themselves with Augustus. As Barbara Levick points out, it was natural for the Flavians to invoke Augustus not only as the founder of the imperial mode of government but also for reasons of dynastic legitimacy.[21] General parallels between Augustus's and Vespasian's ascensions to power included their shared "obligation" to keep the incapable from rising to tyranny, which led to their own accessions as emperor. Although both became emperors through civil war, both presented their legitimacy and rise through military distinction and success in foreign wars. Vespasian and Titus lived in more modest houses than Nero, following Augustus's model. Even Domitian's palace on the Palatine Hill—although quite large—was restricted to that hill and evoked a connection with Augustus, who had lived there during his reign. Vespasian's building program, continued by Titus and Domitian, attempted to restore some degree of pre-Neronian normalcy, as in the restoration of the intersection of roads at the Meta Sudans and the construction of that fountain on top of an Augustan monument that was there prior to the Neronian transformation. The Meta Sudans drew unsubtle parallels between Augustus's dynastic ambitions and the Flavian plan for Rome.

Much of Vespasian's coinage pulled iconographic inspiration from Augustan themes and prototypes and made visual parallels between the two. Some coins of Vespasian depicted the Altar of Providence (Ara Providentia); *providentia* in Latin is strongly associated with the notion of foresight. In the Roman world, this altar and the imperial concept of *providentia* were especially linked with dynastic succession. Coins of Tiberius, Augustus's first successor, depicted the Ara Providentia. On the obverse of these was a portrait of the Deified Augustus, while the altar appeared on the reverse. The altar honored Augustus's foresight through the foundation of a dynasty and by naming Tiberius as his heir. Flavian coins depicting the altar thus communicated that Vespasian was both a successor of Augustus and a founder of a dynasty not dissimilar to Augustus.[22] A series of coins struck under the Flavians also celebrated victory in Judaea with the text "IVDAEA CAPTA" (Judaea Captured), labeling images such as a Jewish captive with a trophy or a dejected female personification of Judaea with an image of the triumphant emperor on either side of a palm tree. The "*Capta* types" drew on Augustan models, making further visual links between the military successes of Augustus and the Flavian emperors.

Vespasian rebuilt the stage in the Theater of Marcellus, a building erected in the reign of Augustus; Cassius Dio also says that Vespasian left the names of the original patrons and did not put his own name on buildings when he restored them, a practice modeled on that of Augustus.[23] The theme of peace is widespread on Vespasian's coinage and in his public building program, which echoes the theme on Augustan coinage, in Augustan building and art, and in the literature of his age. Vespasian's Temple of Peace was placed next to the Forum of Augustus (prior to Domitian's insertion of another imperial forum between the two) and recalled the similar notion of peace that was marked by Augustus's Altar of Peace, as both celebrated the conclusion of foreign wars after major military victories. Vespasian and Augustus both closed the doors of the Temple of Janus to signify that peace. To make the associations even more overt, the architectural style and decorative schemes in Vespasian's Temple of Peace took cues from Augustan architecture.[24] Titus was closely aligned with Augustus in Suetonius's biography of him.[25]

Domitian's reign also saw a continuation of his father's and brother's ideological program, associating the Flavian dynasty with the "good" Julio-Claudians. As Augustus had done in his building program, Domitian too refurbished numerous temples. He began work on an imperial forum between the Temple of Peace and the Forum of Augustus that was nearly completed by the time of his assassination in 96 CE; the immediate proximity of the forum to Augustus's is undoubtedly suggestive. Augustus had built a wooden *stadium*, a type of building for the use of footraces and Greek-style athletic competitions, in the Campus Martius; Domitian built a permanent *stadium* in the Campus Martius, linking him forever with Augustus's memory.[26] Architectural and ideological connections between the Stadium of Domitian and the Circus Maximus, which Caesar and Augustus had monumentalized, further associated Domitian with the founder of the empire, and the new *stadium* continued the Flavian program of specialized buildings for spectacles.[27] A popular social spot in Rome today, Piazza Navona, rests on top of the Stadium of Domitian, and visitors can see the outline of the *cavea* and superstructure of the *stadium* in the surrounding buildings, while the piazza itself lies on top of the area of what had been the track; parts of the ancient structure are accessible below a building on the edge of Piazza Navona. The travertine façade of Domitian's *stadium* quoted the façade of the Colosseum, which evoked the memory of Augustus. Next to the Tiber River, Domitian excavated a massive *naumachia* for the staging of large-scale naval battles, as Augustus had done.[28] Domitian also adjusted and refurbished the Horologium of Augustus, a cosmic calendar in the Campus Martius in a complex consisting of the Augustan Altar of Peace and the Mausoleum of Augustus.[29] An obelisk Augustus had taken from Egypt, one of several he brought to Rome after Egypt's annexation, acted as the sundial. Domitian, as had Augustus, erected an obelisk. As *pontifex maximus*, the high priest of the Roman state religion, Domitian instituted and enforced many moral laws, following Augustus's model.

As with other elements of the Flavian building program, the Colosseum itself, in which all three emperors had a hand, unquestionably bore strong associations with the memory of Augustus. Nero's Domus Aurea had blurred the distinction between public and private, and urban and rural; this subverted the traditional social order, as the lower classes had an unprecedented level of access to the emperor at the edge of the Forum Romanum, the seat of Roman government. The decision to build the Colosseum on Nero's great lake, in the heart of that palace complex, was a brilliant strategy for winning the approval of the people and simultaneously reinforcing customary social order: the amphitheater was a traditional form of Roman public building that asserted social distinctions among spectators. The Flavians did not have to take anything away from the people by choosing to build the amphitheater there, but they did reestablish the original Augustan form of social precedence and hierarchy through the seating arrangements based on the Augustan *Lex Julia Theatralis*.

In the Colosseum's façade, we see a progression of architectural orders, from bottom to top, of the Tuscan, Ionic, and Corinthian orders, which had not characterized any previous amphitheater. Katherine Welch has suggested that the presence of Greek architectural orders in the Colosseum's façade may be linked with the executions staged as mythological enactments that took place in the amphitheater and the Romanization of Greek theatrical performances after Nero's death.[30] Nero had popularized Greek entertainments and performances during his reign through his patronage of music, theater, and athletics, but in the Flavian amphitheater performances of Greek myth ended in the violent and spectacular death of a condemned criminal during midday. The resemblance of the Colosseum's façade to that of theaters in Rome, such as the Theater of Marcellus (figure 3.8), where the façade progresses from Doric on the first level, Ionic on the second, and Corinthian above that, and where Greek plays would have taken place, thus put a uniquely Roman spin on those Greek entertainments and elevated Roman blood sport to the same high cultural level of the theater, according to Welch's interpretation.

Nevertheless, whether any Roman spectator would have thought so deeply about such overly subtle symbolism in the architectural orders on the Colosseum's façade and interpreted them in this way is doubtful. Even if it were the intent of the Colosseum's architects, any message in the architectural design would require intelligibility to be successful. In Rome, before the Colosseum's construction, this progression of orders on building façades had already appeared on theaters, as in the Theater of Marcellus, built in the reign of Augustus.[31] Here, there is a resemblance to the Colosseum's façade, for arched entrances and arcades in the upper levels pierce it, and there is an upward progression of architectural orders. A simpler and perhaps more apt reading of the architectural façade of the Colosseum is that it echoed the façade of Augustan-era theater building. Vespasian had already restored the Augustan Theater of Marcellus, making the monument fresh in the minds of citizens living in Vespasian's Rome, and the similarity of the façades of both buildings would have evoked continuity with the Augustan era in the reign of the Flavians.[32]

Figure 3.8. The façade of the Theater of Marcellus. Note that although the third level is not preserved today, architectural fragments confirm the use of Corinthian order there. (Photograph: Nathan T. Elkins, 2017)

The influence of Augustan-era architectural decoration was also quite apparent in Vespasian's Temple of Peace, completed before the Colosseum and just a short walk from it. Around the Colosseum, there were Flavian buildings that championed the dynasty's military victories in Judaea, namely the Temple of Peace and the Arch of Titus. The construction of the Colosseum *ex manubis* (from the spoils of war), attested by the dedicatory inscription, is also reminiscent of the Augustan-era Amphitheater of Statilius Taurus, which was similarly built from the spoils of Taurus's African campaign. The shields at the top of the Colosseum's façade and the *quadrigae* above the entrances that resembled triumphal arches, and potentially the presence of a sculpture group showing the emperor and a defeated Jewish captive beneath a tree, communicated Flavian victory in the Jewish Revolt just as Augustan monuments similarly trumpeted his own foreign successes. Indeed, Suetonius says that Vespasian's construction of the Colosseum fulfilled a vision that Augustus never realized: an amphitheater in the heart of Rome.[33]

Religious activity that took place in the Colosseum also linked the Flavians with Augustus and Claudius, reinforcing the legitimacy of their claim to power as worthy successors. A plethora of evidence proves that theaters and the Circus Maximus in Rome were home to religious processions and viewing areas for images and attributes of the gods and of the deified emperors to "watch" the games. Outside of Rome, archaeology and inscriptions further attest the presence of religious processions and images in circuses, theaters, and amphitheaters; amphitheaters in particular had strong associations with emperor worship, as games were routinely held for occasions such as the emperor's birthday or on the anniversary of a deified emperor's death.[34]

Indeed, the idea that games and spectacles were secular events or "just for fun" is a modernizing concept and would have been foreign in the Greek and Roman worlds, where all games and festivals had a religious impetus. In early Roman history, slaves or prisoners of war were made to fight to the death during funeral games to honor dead noblemen. Even during the empire, when some dismissively say that the games served a propagandistic function to win popular favor, arena games continued to be offered only on religious occasions and especially during holidays associated with the emperors and their families. The Latin word for gladiatorial combats, *munera* (singular: *munus*), carries the sense of a religious duty or obligation. During the age of Augustus, *munera* were held for the dedication of the Temple of the Deified Julius Caesar, for the inauguration of the Amphitheater of Statilius Taurus, in games for the health of Octavian Caesar (*ludi pro valetudine Caesaris*), in honor of Tiberius's deceased father, in honor of Tiberius's deceased grandfather, for the dedication of the Temple of Quirinus, for the *Quinquatrus* (perhaps for Augustus's rise to *pontifex maximus*), for the death of Agrippa, in games in 11 BCE when Augustus returned to Rome, in commemoration of Agrippa, for the dedication of the Temple of Mars Ultor, and in honor of Drusus (the deceased father of Claudius and Germanicus).[35] It is apparent that each of these occasions held religious significance, and most were often associated with the living emperor or the deaths of members of the imperial family.

Similarly, documentary evidence from Pompeii shows that occasions in honor of the emperor or an imperial family member and the worship of deified emperors were primary reasons for holding *munera* there, often sponsored by priests of the imperial cult.[36] Indeed, early Christian condemnations of amphitheaters do not focus so much on the violence and deaths that took place in the arena as they do on the amphitheater as a place of worship, or what they characterize as a place of idolatry and an abode for demons. Tertullian, for example, criticizes idols of "dead men" in the amphitheater, a reference to images of deified emperors or deceased members of the imperial family.[37]

As discussed in chapter 2, the Colosseum had a *pulvinar* on the southern side of the podium on the short axis, which is analogous to the presence of similar structures in the Circus Maximus, theaters, and *naumachiae* in Rome and to entertainment buildings outside of Rome. Upon that *pulvinar*, sacred images and attributes of the divine were placed to watch the spectacles.[38] In the various entertainment buildings in Rome and elsewhere, a day of games began with a religious procession, and so would a day of games at the Colosseum. Literary evidence for processions and a *pulvinar* in the Colosseum comes from Cassius Dio, describing an eccentricity of Commodus, who fancied himself the reincarnation of Hercules: "As for the lion-skin and club, in the street they were carried before him, and in the amphitheatre they were placed on a gilded chair, whether he was present or not."[39] We might deduce that the laurel crown on a chair (figure 2.23), following the model of Julius Caesar in the theaters, was the typical emblem of the emperor placed in the amphitheater, whether he was present or not; literary descriptions of this may not survive because routine actions are often overlooked in ancient sources in favor of sensational stories of aberrations, such as Commodus's deviant procession and attributes described by Dio.

Amphitheater processions are depicted in relief sculptures from some Italian amphitheaters, allowing us to interpret the mechanics of these processions as rather similar to the processions that preceded a day of games in the Circus Maximus (the *pompa circensis*). Attendants in the amphitheater processions carried stretchers bearing images of gods, goddesses, and deified emperors and family members, while horse-drawn carriages would have transported *exuviae* (attributes). After entering the arena floor, the images and attributes in the Colosseum's procession would have been transferred to the *pulvinar* to "watch" the spectacles, just as they were in the Circus Maximus.

Some of the attributes of gods, goddesses, and the deified emperors and empresses and a laurel crown perhaps representing the living emperor appear on chairs and draped seats on coins of Titus and also early in Domitian's reign, at the time of the Colosseum's inauguration and its first games (e.g., figures 2.22–2.23). One might wonder why the gods on the *pulvinar* were celebrated on the coinage at the time of the Colosseum's dedication. An answer may be found in the other parts of Titus's coinage program and in a curious delay in Vespasian's deification. Quite unusual is the fact that the coinage of Titus does not announce the deification of his father immediately upon his death; instead, the coins only mark the deification six months or more after he had passed away. When the coins did announce Vespasian's deification, they were struck alongside the "restoration"

series of coins on which designs from the coinage of well-remembered predecessors were revived. Coins with designs produced under Augustus, Tiberius
(for the Deified Augustus), and Claudius all went into circulation again and are
distinguishable from the originals by the texts around their designs that translate "restored under Titus." Images on the coins celebrating Vespasian's ascension to divine status with texts like "DIVVS AVGVSTVS VESPASIANVS" (The
Deified Vespasian Augustus) were in the same pockets with coins bearing "DIVVS
AVGVSTVS PATER" (The Deified Augustus, Father), using the precedent of
Augustus for Vespasian's deification and aligning them both ideologically and as
founders of dynasties, just as Vespasian had been linked with Augustus while
he was alive. These coins also appear alongside the coins depicting attributes
and chairs on the *pulvinar* and the Colosseum coins of Titus, which suggests the
strong and logical possibility that the very first games in the Colosseum, the 100
days of games, were staged to honor Vespasian and to celebrate his deification.[40]

Citizens would wear clothing that signified their social rank and status in
society at the games. For instance, senators would wear the *toga* with the broad
purple stripe, while plebeian citizens would wear the *toga* if they had one or,
instead, the *pullus*. Although amphitheater games were a form of entertainment,
they were still sacred and civic events that demanded decorum and seriousness.
Nevertheless, if these first games in the Colosseum were for the Deified Vespasian, citizens may have dressed differently to reflect the seriousness of the spectacles. Cassius Dio claims that on one occasion the emperor Commodus asked
the senators to come to the Colosseum in equestrian dress and in woolen cloaks,
something that they would never do except when an emperor had died.[41] This
request raised the spirits of Dio and his fellow senators, for they thought they
might finally be free of Commodus. This passage suggests that people were expected to dress a certain way for games in the amphitheater when an emperor
died and that, as late as the end of the second century CE, the Colosseum was
the venue for funerary games for an emperor, suggesting also the strong possibility that the first games were staged to celebrate Vespasian's deification.
Other contemporary coins for the Deified Vespasian show his statue carried by
a chariot, drawn by elephants; this is his chariot that would participate in the
processions in the Circus Maximus and in the amphitheater.

Flavian art, architecture, literature, and religion had all come together to promote the idea of Flavian legitimacy and positive links with the Julio-Claudian
past. Vespasian's building program sought to restore Rome to its pre-Neronian
form and actively promoted the memories of Augustus and Claudius. Titus and
Domitian continued the alignment of their images with these two emperors.

The Colosseum itself evoked an association with Augustus through its façade that recalled the Augustan past, and its realization was portrayed as the fulfillment of a vision that Augustus had. Inside the Colosseum itself, religious activity associated with emperor worship, as well as the display of images and attributes of the deified Julio-Claudians alongside those of the Deified Vespasian, signaled that Vespasian's achievements and vision had indeed met, if not exceeded, the accomplishments of his predecessors, for he too was now a god.

On the first day of the inaugural games in the Colosseum, Titus sat in his viewing box in full view of tens of thousands of Romans from all walks of life. Those spectators saw him directly across the arena from the *pulvinar* with images and attributes of the Deified Augustus and the Deified Claudius, and perhaps other revered members of the Julio-Claudian dynasty, such as Germanicus, or even Titus's own childhood friend, Britannicus. Also on that *pulvinar* was the newest god: the Deified Vespasian, for Titus was now the son of a god. The living emperor across from the deified emperors signaled to all who saw it that Titus was the natural and worthy successor to those who came before him—Augustus, Claudius, and Vespasian—and that he too might hope to be a god. After the procession entered the amphitheater and delivered the gods to their place to watch the day of games, Titus and the crowd took their seats and the 100 days of games began to honor the newest god as the sands of the new amphitheater received their first blood.

-IV-

A Hundred Days of Games

IN 80 CE, the emperor Titus inaugurated the great amphitheater that his father had begun with 100 days of games in the city of Rome.[1] It is often assumed that Titus's games took place exclusively in the Colosseum. While the games appropriately began there, on other days spectacles were offered in different venues, as was often the case during long festivals in ancient Rome. This also suggests that the games were held for a purpose greater than the mere celebration of a new entertainment building. The use of different venues for Titus's 100 days of games is clear in Cassius Dio's passage on the subject. He describes in general terms games in the Colosseum, as well as races that would have taken place in the Circus Maximus, an infantry battle, and a large-scale naval battle that Titus staged in the Naumachia of Augustus and other spectacles that took place there before remarking that the emperor's games continued for 100 days. Indeed, we must expect that the long period of games also included multiple sacrifices at temples and performances in the theaters. This lengthy celebration with games was probably in honor of Vespasian's consecration as a god, for games always had a religious impetus and were never a secular affair.

There was a specific program for a day of games in the amphitheater that was followed under the rule of the emperors. That program was the *munus legitimum*, the "proper *munus*," which joined animal hunts and fights between animals with gladiatorial combats and goes back to the age of Augustus; animal spectacles had been a common feature of entertainments in Roman circuses, and they continued to be held there, although animal spectacles in the amphitheater now preceded gladiatorial combats. After the procession into the arena at the start of a day of games in the amphitheater, the morning hours featured exhibitions of hunting prowess and the pitting of animals against one another. At the midday, respectable citizens left the arena to rest and to have lunch, while others remained to watch the gruesome executions of condemned criminals. In the afternoon, gladiators took center stage. A day of spectacles at the Colosseum required not only elaborate productions but their successful staging as well.

The *Pompa*

Preceding a day of amphitheater games was the procession, or *pompa*.[2] Italian relief sculptures provide good evidence for the composition of the processions. In a relief from the necropolis at the Stabian Gate in Pompeii, the ceremonial bodyguard of a magistrate, the *lictores*, head the procession along with trumpeters, indicative of the festiveness of these ostentatious *pompae*. Following them are armorers and attendants carrying gladiatorial weaponry. After that is an attendant holding a tablet who functioned as a sort of announcer at the games; another attendant carries a palm branch, a symbol of victory awarded to victorious gladiators. Beyond them is the *editor* wearing his *toga*, and behind him are attendants carrying the shields and helmets of the gladiators who would fight that day. Gladiators would typically participate in these processions also and are often depicted on these reliefs, as on a relief from Amiternum in Italy. At the end of the procession on the relief from Pompeii is another trumpeter and attendants leading horses that are presumably those that would be mounted by gladiators known as *equites*. This relief sculpture is no doubt abbreviated in terms of its content, as are most "historical" Roman relief sculptures. We may expect that tame or at least trained animals also participated in amphitheater processions. Condemned prisoners may have been paraded in the *pompa* as well. Martial records that informers were paraded before the crowd during Flavian games in the Colosseum, an act designed to publicly humiliate them before exile.[3] Dancers and acrobats enlivened processions in other venues and may also have been present in amphitheater processions.

Other reliefs, as at Amiternum and Capua, show us images of the gods that were carried on stretchers, *fercula* (singular: *ferculum*), and carts that carried the attributes of gods. These carts were called *tensae* (singular: *tensa*) for masculine deities and *carpenta* (singular: *carpentum*) for feminine deities. The carts used in amphitheater processions are analogous to the carts used in the Circus

Maximus, many of which appear on Roman imperial coins in the first century CE for honored members of the imperial family. Once the procession entered the amphitheater, attendants would transfer these images and attributes to pre-prepared draped seats or chairs on the *pulvinar*, as they did in the Circus Maximus. The *pompa* not only provided an entertaining spectacle but served an important religious function in bringing the gods to the amphitheater.

The presence of the *editor* in many depictions of the amphitheater procession is significant and would provide a precedent for the emperor to participate, at least on occasion, in processions in the Colosseum. After all, the emperor was the sponsor of games in the Colosseum, and most certainly during the inaugural games. Indeed, Cassius Dio, a contemporary of Commodus, describes Commodus's participation in a procession to the amphitheater, in which the lion skin and club are carried before him and placed on a chair there.[4] Suetonius says that Augustus led a procession in the Circus Maximus while being carried in a litter because he was ill.[5] After the procession and in full view of the spectators, *editores* ceremonially examined the weapons with which the gladiators were to fight that day to make sure they were sufficiently sharp. The Pompeii relief includes in its representation of the *pompa* the weapons that the *editor* would examine. Emperors also examined the weapons to be used in the Colosseum. Suetonius records that when two nobles were found guilty of conspiring to usurp Titus, the emperor elected not to dispatch them but invited them to dinner and to a gladiatorial spectacle, where he seated the men near him, so that when the weapons were presented to him for examination he passed them instead to the two conspirators; Nerva similarly placed a conspirator next to him at a spectacle and handed the swords presented for inspection over to them.[6] After the completion of the *pompa*, and after the gods had taken their seats, the crowd probably applauded and cheered as they all took their seats to watch the day of spectacles, which began with animal sports.

The *Venationes*

The first spectacles of the day, after the *pompa* and lasting until midday, were the *venationes* (singular: *venatio*), animal spectacles, more specifically hunts.[7] Before they were joined with amphitheater spectacles in Rome, *venationes* were held in the Circus Maximus and were usually stand-alone events at public festivals, the *ludi*. Exotic animals were first introduced to the city of Rome by means of Roman military expansion and overseas conquest in the period of the Middle Republic, when animals from foreign lands were displayed in Rome during triumphal processions. Citizens first saw elephants in Rome, for example, when the beasts, after being captured from Pyrrhus's army, were marched in a triumphal parade in 275 BCE.[8] The first recorded staged animal hunt was in 186 BCE and involved panthers and lions.[9] Katherine Welch links the origin of animal spectacles with the Roman army, as she does also with the origins of gladiatorial combats and amphitheaters in the Republic.[10] She points out that wild beasts were often deployed in military contexts to execute captured enemies and deserters in the most gruesome and brutal ways. For example, at games in Greece, Lucius Aemilius Paullus had deserters from his own army trampled by elephants in 167 BCE; Scipio Aemilianus sent deserters and prisoners of war to Rome to be thrown to the beasts at public shows in 146 BCE.[11] Animals were often involved in public executions, even well into the period of the emperors.

Hunts involving man versus beast usually featured exotic and dangerous animals, such as leopards and other large cats imported from Roman territories in North Africa. The hunt of a formidable prey animal made it an exciting spectacle for the crowds to watch, for the hunter would usually win, but on occasion the beast might kill him. There is some evidence from the Roman world that crowds sometimes sympathized with and rooted for animals, although one usually expected their deaths during hunts.[12] Elaborate stages that mimicked jungles, forests, and hills, quickly erected by means of the elevators in *hypogea*, added to the drama and suspense of the hunt, and to the unpredictability of the outcome, as the hunter might become the hunted.

There is a plethora of mosaics and other visual media from Italy and the provinces attesting to the popularity of hunting spectacles. One example is the Magerius Mosaic, which was discovered in Smirat, Tunisia, and which was made in the third century CE (figure 4.1). The mosaic celebrates an extraordinary hunt in a local amphitheater and the remarkable generosity of the sponsor of the games, Magerius. The mosaic was probably in the dining room of Magerius's villa. On the two long edges of the mosaic are victorious hunters spearing leopards; the names of the hunters are written below them (Spittara, Bullarius, Hilarinus, and Mamertinus), as are the names of the defeated leopards (Victor, Crispinus, Luxurius, and Romanus), which may also be something of a joke. For instance, Victor is certainly not the victor, and a true Roman (Romanus) would never die in the arena. The theatricality of some hunts is evident in the representation of Spittara, who stands on stilts as he dispatches his leopard. Along the short edges of the mosaic are representations of the goddess Diana, appropriate in the context of a hunt, and the god Dionysus. The large figure who is only partially preserved in one quadrant of the mosaic is probably a representation of

Figure 4.1. The Magerius Mosaic, depicting hunting scenes in commemoration of *venationes* sponsored by Magerius, third century CE, from Smirat, Tunisia (© Vanni Archive/Art Resource, NY)

Magerius himself; above his head is the word "MAGERI," which is also repeated next to Diana on the other side of the mosaic. Magerius's name appears in the vocative case, representing the crowd's acclamations of him as they called his name. The center of the mosaic shows an attendant holding four moneybags stamped ∞, which symbolizes that each bag contains 1,000 *denarii*, an extraordinary sum of money. The inscriptions around the figure provide the significance of the event to which we are witness. A herald calls for the troupe of hunters to be paid 500 *denarii* for each leopard killed, and the crowd looks to Magerius, who on account of his generosity, doubled it and paid 1,000 *denarii* per leopard.

Human combatants in the *venationes* were either *venatores* (singular: *venator*) or *bestiarii* (singular: *bestiarius*), which respectively translate to "hunter" and "beast man" (i.e., "beast fighter"). There is some disagreement on what distinguished a *venator* from a *bestiarius*, but according to Roger Dunkle's study of the subject and his attention to visual representations of *venationes*, they differ according to their armament and status.[13] The *venator* was equipped in a manner similar to a professional hunter outside the arena, wearing a tunic and with a thrusting spear and a throwing spear as his weaponry. This light weaponry and clothing made him quick and agile, which would be necessary for success when facing tigers, leopards, lions, or the like. *Venatores* were also professionally trained for the task of hunting wild beasts; in the first century BCE, many of them were imported to Rome from the same areas as the animals that they were tasked to hunt, suggesting they had experience with the beasts in question. For instance, when crocodiles first appeared in Rome's arena, they were accompanied by trained crocodile hunters who also came from Egypt.[14]

Pompey, Julius Caesar's rival, staged an elephant hunt and brought *venatores* from what is modern Algeria for that event.[15] Gradually, the importation of *venatores* seems to have waned, and by the time of the dedication of the Colosseum *venatores* were trained in special schools, as were gladiators, and typically would be sold as slaves to those schools with the purpose of entering that profession. One of the four schools that Domitian built near the Colosseum was the Ludus Matutinus (the Morning School), which implies that slaves were professionally trained there to hunt wild beasts. *Bestiarii*, in Dunkle's interpretation, were equipped like gladiators: they wore similar armor, including large helmets, and carried swords. Dunkle speculates that in the early days a *bestiarius* was a gladiator put into a *venatio*. In texts from the period of the Roman Empire, *bestiarii* are linked with those who were to be executed as the midday entertainment. In many instances, condemned criminals thrown to the beasts would be given a sword or some other weapon of substandard quality to make the death more interesting to watch, although the victim's lack of training with the deficient blade would guarantee the expected outcome.

Dunkle's interpretation of the difference between the two is not universally accepted; other scholars view *bestiarii* as assistants to the professional hunters, the *venatores*. In this interpretation, they cared for the animals prior to the spectacles, and they may have provoked the animals before and during a show or execution to increase their ferocity.[16] Others understand *bestiarii* as professional fighters who engaged in single combats with wild beasts. Defying typical expectations, hunters could sometimes be women, as indicated by one of Martial's epigrams where he describes a woman who felled a lion in one of the Colosseum's early spectacles and compares her feat with Hercules's slaying of the Nemean lion; Cassius Dio also mentions the involvement of women during the *venationes* in the Colosseum's inaugural games over which Titus presided.[17]

It is difficult to discuss specific hunts that occurred during Titus's 100 days of games in the Colosseum, for there is debate as to whether Martial's *Book of Spectacles* describes events from the inaugural games held by Titus, games held by Domitian, or a mixture of spectacles held by both emperors. Ambiguity pervades these epigrams because Martial addresses the emperor only as "Caesar" throughout; the use of godlike epithets and characteristics ascribed to the emperor might suggest Domitian, although Titus cannot be discounted. T. V. Buttrey pointed out that a rhinoceros features in the epigrams and appears on Domitianic coins of circa 83 CE and after (figure 4.2), suggesting a Domitianic date for the *Book of Spectacles*, as rhinoceroses appeared only very rarely at amphitheater games in Rome on account of their massive size, their difficulty to capture and transport, and their resultant expense.[18] In view of this, rhinoceroses, therefore, appeared in multiple exhibitions against other animals and were not often killed. While it is a provocative suggestion to dismiss the association of the *Book of Spectacles* with the inaugural games of Titus on account of the evidence of Domitian's coins, it is possible that the rhinoceros on Domitian's coins appeared in Titus's games of 80 CE and that the beast either was still used in spectacles early in Domitian's reign or was simply a second animal. Whatever the case, it is sufficient for our purposes to note that Martial was an eyewitness to some of the earliest games held in the Colosseum; his testimony

Figure 4.2. A small copper coin (*quadrans*) of Domitian from circa 83 CE, or after, depicting on its obverse a rhinoceros; the reverse depicts "S C" (by decree of the Senate) surrounded by the emperor's titles, which provide the approximate date. (Courtesy of the American Numismatic Society, 1944.100.54620)

provides a sense of what the earliest games were like under the Flavian emperors, whether they were held by Titus or Domitian. A cycle of three epigrams describes a pregnant sow that was hit by a spear during a *venatio* and gave birth on the spot but also died from the wound.[19] Other epigrams describe the successful exploits of Carpophorus, a beast fighter, in the Colosseum; he killed a boar, speared a charging bear, felled a large lion, and dispatched a panther from a distance; his achievements are compared with those of Hercules.[20]

In addition to hunts involving men and wild beasts, the Romans also enjoyed watching animals hunt one another. Letting dogs loose to hunt and kill deer or hares was particularly popular. More remarkable and entertaining for the Romans was pitting large beasts against one another in mortal combat; oftentimes these would involve animals that would never encounter one another in the wild. Cassius Dio mentions a battle between cranes and an engagement involving four elephants at the inaugural games of Titus.[21] The rhinoceros appears in two of Martial's epigrams, easily and spectacularly dispatching various large animals. In the first instance, he says: "The rhinoceros displayed all around the arena, Caesar, has delivered combat that it did not promise. Launching itself headlong it flared up into such a terrible rage! What a great bull that was, for which a bull was but a toy!" In the second, he writes:

While the trainers were nervously worrying a rhinoceros and the great beast's temper was taking a long time to gather strength, men began to give up hope of any battles ensuing in the conflict that they had been promised. But finally the rage that we had known earlier returned, for he picked up a heavy bear on his double horn like a bull tossing a load of dummies to the stars. . . . He scooped up a pair of bullocks on his pliable neck, the ferocious aurochs and the bison gave in to him; a lion trying to escape from him raced full tilt into the spears: go now, spectators, and carp at sluggish delays![22]

Martial also mentions a fight between an elephant and a bull, and the mauling of a lion by a tiger.[23]

Animals who appeared at the games need not always be forced into violent combats or hunts. Some animals, under the supervision of a trainer, performed tricks for the audience. One of Martial's epigrams tells of a performing lion that had attacked its trainer in the Colosseum and that the emperor subsequently ordered to be killed for the offense.[24] Another epigram describes a bear who was "rolling headlong" when it was ensnared in glue, used to trap birds; Kathleen Coleman interprets this unusual epigram as a performing bear that was doing somersaults, perhaps in something like a barrel, when it got ensnared in the equipment or when it simply lost footing in the blood-soaked sand, which caused

Martial to use the metaphor of glue for a bird trap.[25] Two other passages, potentially related to one another, refer to a domesticated bull raised aloft in the arena by means of some contraption; the second passage cites the myth of Europa, as a man named Alcides is carried aloft on the back of the emperor's bull.[26]

By the time the Colosseum was built, there was a robust and professionalized network that supplied exotic animals from the Roman provinces and beyond to Italy and Rome to appear in arena spectacles.[27] Several mosaics in the provinces attest to the logistics of the capture of animals for the games. The danger and difficulties of transporting wild animals from the point of capture to Rome made *venationes* costly. Cassius Dio claims that 9,000 wild and domestic animals were slaughtered during Titus's inaugural games, a most ostentatious display of wealth and extravagance.[28] The number is probably exaggerated, but one must wonder what became of the carcasses of the scores of animals killed in the arena on any given day of games.

Meat was an expensive luxury for most Romans and not as prominent in their diet as it is in modern, Western diets. During public festivals, the meat from sacrificial animals was distributed to the people as part of the celebration. It would seem wasteful for pragmatic Romans simply to discard the meat of animals killed at the games. Indeed, the early Christian author Tertullian alludes to the Roman practice of butchering and consuming animals killed in the amphitheater.[29] In Rome, animal bones found in the drains below the Colosseum and also excavated in the Meta Sudans seem to confirm that the crowds feasted at midday or in the afternoon on the meat of animals killed during the morning spectacles.[30] The meats would have been prepared near the Colosseum where they would have been available for purchase or perhaps even distributed freely to the spectators. Recent excavations at Carnuntum, in modern Austria, have yielded evidence of bakeries and fast-food stands next to the amphitheater. Around that area were also shops that sold souvenirs related to the games in the amphitheater, such as oil lamps with gladiators on them.[31] The availability of food and drink at the Colosseum is something to which spectators in modern stadiums can relate, although our sources of meat at such venues are very different. Following the model of Carnuntum, we may reasonably posit that souvenirs, such as oil lamps with scenes of *venationes*, executions, or various types of gladiators, were sold in the immediate vicinity of the Colosseum during the games, which is not dissimilar to the availability of memorabilia available at events in modern sports stadiums, or even the Colosseum-related kitsch and knickknacks peddled to tourists near the Colosseum today, nearly 2,000 years after the building's inauguration.

Executions Staged as Mythological Enactments

After the conclusion of the morning's animal spectacles, executions of condemned criminals took place at midday, the *meridianum spectaculum*. At this time, respectable citizens, prior to the gladiatorial combats in the afternoon, might retire from the amphitheater for a break and perhaps have lunch outside the arena. Nonetheless, many spectators stayed for the particularly gruesome events. As Welch argued, animal spectacles were linked with the military's punishment of deserters and prisoners of war in the Middle Republic. This type of Roman punishment, whereby beasts provided the agency behind the execution, is known as *damnatio ad bestias*, "condemnation to the beasts." This Roman form of execution is familiar to many modern people through early Christian martyr tales, such as that of Perpetua and Felicitas, who are said to have been thrown to the beasts in the amphitheater at Carthage, located in modern Tunisia. Other forms of execution included forcing the condemned to fight in mock naval battles in the *naumachiae*, crucifixion, and burning alive. Crucifixions, a punishment particularly favored for use on slaves, often took place in entertainment venues, including amphitheaters, as indicated by a painted advertisement at Pompeii that publicized games in Cumae: "twenty pairs of gladiators, crucifixions, a hunt, and awnings."[32] Christian tradition holds that Peter was crucified on an inverted cross in 64 CE in the Circus of Gaius and Nero on Vatican Hill, where St. Peter's Basilica now stands. The spectacle of a crucifixion could be enhanced by allowing animals to maul the restrained victim, or by lighting the crucified on fire. Death by burning is called *damnatio ad flammas*, "condemnation by fire." In the Colosseum, executions incorporated *damnatio ad bestias*, *damnatio ad flammas*, crucifixion, or some combination thereof, although they were often also staged as mythological enactments, or what Coleman calls "fatal charades."[33]

Most people who died in the Colosseum were condemned criminals, not gladiators. Gladiators were professionally trained to fight in high-stakes combat and thus expensive to prepare and maintain, which means their deaths came at great financial cost. In the Roman penal system, one could be condemned to a gladiator school or a hunting school (*damnatio ad ludum gladiatorium* or *damnatio ad ludum venatorium*). Condemnation to train as a gladiator or *venator* was a merciful punishment when compared with *damnatio ad bestias*, *damnatio ad flammas*, or crucifixion, as it allowed a chance for survival and hope to buy or win one's eventual freedom. One could also be condemned to the mines, in which one suffered a brutal life of hard labor and poor treatment until it ended;

condemnation to life as a gladiator was still preferable to this for many people. The worst punishments were the *summa supplicia* (highest punishments), brutal executions that included no hope for survival.

What those executed in the arena and gladiators and *venatores* shared was their status, for they were noncitizens and slaves. Citizens were generally exempted from the suffering and humiliation of *summa supplicia*, or the debasement of condemnation to a gladiator school or the mines. Typically, citizens condemned to death would face swifter, less agonizing, and less humiliating deaths in a private setting. For a citizen, capital punishment was typically beheading (*damnatio ad gladium*, "condemnation to the sword"). Noncitizens, usually slaves or foreigners, who were condemned to die in brutal and humiliating ways were called *noxii* (singular: *noxius*), "convicted criminals"; they might also be called *damnati* (singular: *damnatus*), "condemned."

To many modern people, the different treatment of noncitizens and citizens facing capital punishment by Roman authorities is readily observed in the respective treatment and executions of the Christian figures Jesus, Peter, and Paul. Mocking and humiliation, especially as they relate to one's crime, were important elements in Roman executions of *noxii* or *damnati*. A significant part of the prelude to Jesus's execution was mocking and humiliation related to his crime; he was "king of the Jews," which was a challenge to the authority of the emperor and the Roman government in Judaea. Consequently, after his flagellation, soldiers dressed him in a purple robe and gave him the attributes of a rod and a crown of thorns, all to imitate the dress of a king, and they mocked him. As he was crucified, a sign above his head labeled him "king of the Jews." Peter, also a noncitizen, was crucified on an inverted cross in a public setting in Rome, the Circus of Gaius and Nero. Although Christian tradition holds that it was his desire to be crucified on an inverted cross, since he felt unworthy to die the same way as Jesus, it is far more probable that his cross was inverted at the command of the Roman authorities to mock or humiliate him as a follower of a condemned criminal who was himself crucified. This would have made his execution a farcical spectacle for the Roman crowd. Unlike Peter and Jesus, Paul was a Roman citizen. He was accused of having defiled the Temple in Jerusalem and, as was the right of a citizen, appealed his case to the emperor. He was beheaded privately in Rome, according to Christian tradition.

Roman punishment had as one of its aims retribution, whereby the punishment was equal to the crime. For example, an arsonist might suffer immolation in the arena. Humiliation, as we have seen, was another component of Roman executions. Humiliation alienated the individual from the spectators. Citizen spectators were exempted from the humiliation and extreme suffering they witnessed in the arena at midday, and thus they were united in a feeling of moral superiority as they watched the just punishment, regardless of their social rank, whether senator, equestrian, or plebeian. There may also have been a deterrent component to these gruesome executions performed in the arena. Although citizen spectators were generally exempted from the treatments they saw, slaves and foreigners were also present at the games, and they could suffer such fates if they were convicted of crimes. During the imperial period, evidence suggests plebeians who were convicted of crimes were sometimes stripped of citizenship and subjected to the same brutal punishments as slaves and noncitizens. Executions also acted as spectacular entertainment for the crowds. Thus, executions took many different forms and were never monotonous. Condemned criminals could be shackled together and forced to fight to the death, covered in flammable substances and set alight, placed on an iron chair and fried, or dismembered by horses.

Tertullian, writing in North Africa, describes executions in amphitheaters that were staged as mythological enactments. For instance, he writes of seeing "Attis" castrated and another man who played the role of Hercules burned alive.[34] Coleman interprets the statement about the criminal playing Attis as a form of a "mitigated death penalty." Roman crowds reveled in spectacular humiliation and suffering and in the performances of condemned criminals who might be forced to inflict harm upon themselves. Coleman suggests that this criminal was coerced to play the role of Attis, who according to the myths castrated himself; he may have been spared death in exchange for his act of self-mutilation before the crowds. Epigrams in books 8 and 10 of Martial's *Epigrams* (not to be confused with the epigrams in Martial's *Book of Spectacles*) recount an episode of a "mitigated death penalty" by self-inflicted suffering in the Colosseum during the reign of Domitian: a man, playing the role of Mucius Scaevola from Roman history, burned off his right hand over a fire.[35] To avoid death, the criminal held his hand in a fire until it was burned away. The burning of Hercules in Tertullian's account refers to a *damnatus* assigned to and dressed in the role of Hercules who is subsequently set ablaze, enacting Hercules's own immolation on a pyre and his ascension as a god to Mount Olympus. This form of execution, in which the condemned played the role of Hercules at his immolation, seems to have been rather popular, for numerous other ancient sources describe similar executions enacted in the guise of this myth.

In the Colosseum, we know from Martial's eyewitness account in the *Book of Spectacles* that certain executions took place in either Titus's inaugural games or Domitian's games. The first epigram dealing with an execution tells of a woman, forced into some sort of bestial intercourse with a bull, enacting the myth of Pasiphae who coupled with Poseidon's white bull and gave birth to the half-man, half-bull Minotaur.[36] This was a particularly terrible and humiliating form of *damnatio ad bestias*, whereby the woman would have ultimately been trampled to death by the animal after suffering extreme public humiliation by it. Another execution in the Colosseum appears to have combined crucifixion and *damnatio ad bestias*. Martial writes:

Just as Prometheus, chained on a Scythian crag, fed the tireless bird on his prolific breast, so Laureolus, hanging on no false cross, gave up his defenseless entrails to a Scottish bear. His mangled limbs were still alive, though the parts were dripping with blood, and in his whole body there actually was no body. Then [what heinous crime merited such severe] punishment? Either in his guilt he had stabbed his master in the throat with a sword, or in his madness robbed a temple of its hoard of gold, or stealthily set you alight with brutal torches, Rome. This miscreant had surpassed crimes recounted in tales of old; in his case, what had been legend really was punishment.[37]

Laureolus is not the real name of the *damnatus* but the name of a character from Roman mime, a notorious bandit who suffered crucifixion. In this enactment, the condemned criminal plays the role of Laureolus, crucified in the arena or bound to a pole, when a bear from Caledonia (Scotland) is set loose upon him to facilitate his death. While restrained, he is ultimately shredded by the bear.

Allusions are made to the fate of Prometheus, who in myth was chained to a rock and eternally punished, as his liver regenerated each day only to be devoured by Jupiter's eagle. Prometheus's torture is a subject in the sculptural programs in the amphitheaters at Puteoli and Capua; the myth's relation to divine retribution and to executions performed as mythological enactments probably indicates that similar executions were performed in amphitheaters throughout the Roman Empire. Indeed, a late-Roman period flask in the Römisch-Germanisches Zentralmuseum in Mainz, Germany, shows on its neck a *damnatus* bound in an elevated position to a pole while he is helplessly attacked by a bear, a scene similar to Martial's description of the execution of the condemned criminal in this epigram; the attendant standing nearby may have been the figure responsible for affixing the condemned to the pole, and goading the bear to maul its victim (figure 4.3).

The final lines of the epigram that concern the criminal who plays the role of Laureolus, interrogating the potential crimes of the condemned man, merit some comment. First, Martial and the crowd do not know why he is suffering this horrible fate in the arena; they can only speculate. Second, what is important, in Martial's view, is that he did something to deserve it and that the crowd sees life (and death) imitate art and myth. Such an attitude conveys the sense of moral superiority of the citizen crowd in the collective viewing of noncitizen "others" receiving retribution and punishment, perceiving them to be just and deserved. Martial conveys a similar sentiment in watching a criminal playing the role of Mucius Scaevola, burning off his hand to avoid being executed by fire, in games of Domitian: "After such achievement I would sooner not know what this hand had done before; enough for me to know it as I saw it."[38]

Another epigram in the *Book of Spectacles* states: "Seeing that you are being torn apart like that by a Lucanian bear, Daedalus, how you must wish you had

Figure 4.3. Detail of the neck of a terracotta flask from circa 400 CE depicting a *damnatus* affixed to a pole and mauled by a bear as an attendant stands nearby (Römisch-Germanisches Zentralmuseum, Mainz; Photograph: S. Steidl)

your feathers now!" Coleman understands this criminal as dressed with fake wings and feathers, like Daedalus who in myth fashioned wings to flee his captivity on Crete, but here a bear savaged the grounded criminal.[39] He may also have been suspended from some sort of contraption to simulate flight, which would have amused spectators as the irritated bear continuously pursued and reached for its hesitant victim until it succeeded. Stages for executions could be elaborate. For instance, a platform was erected in Nero's wooden amphitheater for a condemned criminal in the guise of Icarus to be pushed off and to plummet to his death. There is also comic reversal in the execution of "Daedalus" because here, contrary to the myth, "Daedalus" fails; indeed, many of these enactments had farcical elements about them, which would have amused a citizen audience generally impervious to such humiliating deaths.[40] Another epigram tells of Orpheus, who in myth charmed wild and domestic animals, falling to a bear;[41] such a reversal of the myth here is another example of comedic elements during the midday executions.

Gladiatorial Combat

After the conclusion of the *meridianum spectaculum*, which featured executions of the most gruesome sort, anyone who left the amphitheater returned to reclaim his seat for the most anticipated event of the day: the gladiatorial fights.[42] Their origins are debated among scholars, who are essentially divided into two camps. Some argue that gladiatorial games began in the traditions of the Osco-Samnite peoples of Campania, an area south of Rome, who were culturally distinct from the Romans prior to Rome's expansion in the fourth and third centuries BCE. Roman authors speak of the Campanians forcing armed men to fight at their banquets; and, indeed, tomb paintings and some painted pots from southern Italy, dating to the fourth century BCE, show men engaged in one-on-one combat. Others see their origin in Etruria, the area of Italy north of Rome inhabited by the Etruscans, who also had a culture and language distinct from the Romans; they were overcome by the Romans in the fourth and third centuries BCE as well, although they exerted immense cultural influence on early Rome on account of their proximity and trade relations with Rome. Even Rome's last kings were Etruscan, prior to the founding of the Republic in 509 BCE. Etruscan tomb paintings show events that seem to foreshadow Roman blood sports. For instance, in the Tomb of the Augurs, a character identified as Phersu by a painted label holds the leash of a dog, which attacks a man who holds a club and has a bag over his head. This could be an early form of execution by an animal. More probable, in view of the funerary context of the image, the painting depicted a sort of human sacrifice at the funeral of the deceased Etruscan nobleman.

The problem with the Roman literary evidence is that what is said about the origins of gladiatorial games comes from a much later period in Roman history, centuries after Rome expanded into these other areas of Italy. The Romans themselves were not in agreement on where gladiatorial games originated. The first attested gladiatorial games in Rome date to 264 BCE according to Livy, who wrote in the age of Augustus about games sponsored by Marcus and Decimus Brutus for their deceased father.[43] But earlier games may have simply escaped documentation. According to ancient sources, the holding of gladiatorial combats often coincided with funerary memorials, and even in the age of Augustus there was strong correlation of these games with memorials for deceased members of the emperor's family or with holidays associated with the living emperor. *Munus*, which describes a program of gladiatorial games, translates to "duty" or "obligation," so perhaps it reflected the funerary origins of these games in Rome as obligations to honor deceased nobles.

In Latin, *gladiator* (plural: *gladiatores*) literally means "swordsman," for it derives from the word for sword, *gladius*. Gladiators typically entered the profession involuntarily. They were slaves sold to gladiator schools, which in turn trained them to fight in the arena, or they might be criminals spared the fate of capital punishment and instead sentenced to *damnatio ad ludum*. To punish a disobedient slave, his owner might sell him directly to a gladiator school. Prisoners of war could also be sent to gladiator schools. If he fought skillfully and honorably, and survived, a gladiator might hope to buy or win his freedom some years in the future.

Rarely, gladiators were free men who volunteered for the profession. In so doing, these free men essentially sold themselves into slavery, for they became property of the gladiator school, suffered the same training and discipline as other gladiators, and risked dying in the arena in combat, or if the *editor* or *munerarius* commanded it. Gladiators, as did those in many other performative and service professions, possessed *infamia*, a social stigma best translated as "dishonor" or "disgrace." Actors, *venatores*, and prostitutes were among other professions that also possessed *infamia*. One's actions, such as corruption, criminal conviction, or desertion from the army could also cause one to take on this quality. *Infamia* carried with it not only social alienation among respectable citizen society but also legal consequences. For instance, anyone participating in a profession that caused him to bear *infamia* was not allowed to exercise any citizen rights, such as voting, serving on juries, or joining the army. Therefore, volunteering to be a gladiator essentially meant giving up one's citizenship and becoming vulnerable to the harsh and humiliating treatment that slaves and prisoners of war would experience in a gladiator school. For this reason, people from Rome's upper classes did not with any great frequency volunteer to become gladiators. More volunteers would have come from Rome's poorest classes. Citizens who were unable to subsist might find some respite in the guaranteed meals and lodging offered by a gladiator school. Still, some volunteered to fight as gladiators for the attention of the crowds and the small chance of striking it rich as successful gladiators who, after winning their freedom, might run their own gladiator schools.

Indeed, there was a peculiar dichotomy in the Roman regard for gladiators. On the one hand, they were slaves possessing *infamia*: the absolute dregs of Roman society. On the other hand, they were highly regarded for their martial skill, bravery, and talent. The sweat of the most famous gladiators was collected, sold, and used as an aphrodisiac or in cosmetics; this practice may be related to the earlier Greek practice of collecting and selling the sweat of young, toned athletes for medicinal purposes. Gladiators were symbols of virility and sexual fortitude, lusted after by women and men. Graffiti at Pompeii call a certain *retiarius* (a gladiator equipped with a net and trident), named Crescens, "the girls' darling" and "netter of the girls by night." Another gladiator, a heavily armed Thracian named Celadus, is called "girls' heartthrob" and "girls' idol." Other graffiti at Pompeii, and even figural graffiti in the Colosseum itself, attest to the widespread popularity of gladiators.[44]

Many successful gladiators who had earned their freedom went on to become *lanistae* and oversaw gladiator schools themselves or worked as trainers in the gladiator schools. Gladiators experienced a rigorous training regimen in the *ludus*. Drills included striking a wooden pole repeatedly with a wooden sword and shield. They learned specific moves and tactics so that fights in the arena would be among skilled combatants and thus entertaining to watch. On the basis of their skill and winning records, they were divided into hierarchical ranks. Gladiators ate mostly large portions of barely. Barley was both relatively cheap and hearty; large portions were necessary for the high number of calories they expended in training.

The individual cells for gladiators in the *ludus* were quite small. At Pompeii's gladiator school, they are smaller than 4.65 square meters (50 square feet) each. Many gladiators had the freedom to come and go from the *ludus* if they could be trusted. If not, they would be confined to their cells when they were not training or performing, often further restrained by chains attached to the walls. Some gladiators had wives and families that lived with them in the *ludus*.

With their earnings, many gladiators joined burial clubs, so that, when they died, they would receive proper funerals and burial or cremation. Alternatively, their friends and families might pay for their funerals. Tombstones for gladiators have been recovered in different parts of the Roman Empire. Several scholars have attempted to calculate the average life expectancy for gladiators—for example, by using information available on tombstones—but such methods are fraught with problems. What we can say is that, contrary to the perception we may have from Hollywood, gladiators were quite young. Funerary inscriptions often provide the age at death, which is usually in the early to mid-twenties. Many became gladiators even younger; an inscription records one who died at 17.[45]

Gladiators specialized in various fighting styles and tactics appropriate to their armament, and Romans expected certain types of gladiators to fight against one another.[46] Some important types include:

1. *Eques, equites*—"horseman." *Equites* were lightly armed and mounted gladiators, who might fight on horseback or dismount and fight.
2. *Hoplomachus, hoplomachi*—"hoplite." The *hoplomachus* was a heavily armed gladiator whose armament and weaponry mimicked that of a Greek hoplite. He wore a loincloth, armor on his right arm, and tall greaves and carried a small round shield. Instead of a sword, he carried a spear and a small dagger to use as a backup weapon. Representations suggest he wore a brimmed helmet lacking a figural crest. This gladiator type was typically paired against the *thraex* or *murmillo*.
3. *Murmillo, murmillones*. There is no good translation of *murmillo*. It may be related to a Greek word for a specific kind of fish, for this gladiator wore a distinctive helmet with a wide brim and a thick crest that resembles a fin (figure 4.4). *Murmillones* were a popular gladiator type in the imperial period and are some of the most recognizable types of gladiators. The *murmillo* carried a large oblong shield that curved inward to protect the body. He also wore a loincloth, armor on his right arm, and greaves and carried a typical *gladius*, similar to the short sword carried by Roman legionaries. The *murmillo* was typically pitted against the *thraex*, *hoplomachus*, or *retiarius*.
4. *Provocator, provocatores*—"challenger." This gladiator wore a loincloth, a greave on his left leg, and a breastplate that protected only the upper

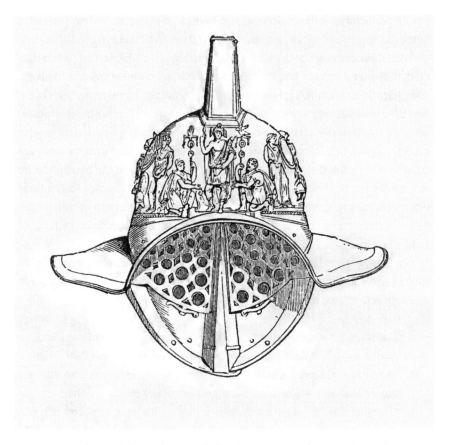

Figure 4.4. The bronze helmet of a *murmillo* found at Pompeii (After *The Illustrated History of the World for the English People: From the Earliest Period to the Present Time*, vol. 1 [London: Ward, Lock, and Co., 1884], 330)

chest. He wore a helmet with a visor and a neck guard at the back, but no brim. His shield was rectangular and convex to offer protection around the body, similar to the Roman legionary's shield. The *provocator* carried a short sword with a straight blade; in art, *provocatores* usually seem to have been paired with other *provocatores* in combat, although a funerary relief in the Yale University Art Gallery shows a *provocator* fighting a *murmillo*.[47]

5. *Retiarius, retiarii*—"net-man." The *retiarius* is quite distinctive in terms of his armament. He had no helmet and carried no shield. Instead, he carried a trident, a dagger as a backup weapon, and a net; he wore armor on his left arm, which terminated at the neck in a ridge to protect

that side of the face and neck from blows, and greaves. Like most other gladiators, he wore a loincloth. The net was used to strip the shield or sword away from his opponent, and then to snare his opponent for a kill at a distance with the trident, or to impede him enough to attack him with the dagger. Crowds either loved or hated *retiarii*. Many found them cowardly and effeminate, for their armament forced them to attack and retreat repeatedly, and they exposed the most flesh of any gladiator. For that same reason, *retiarii* could especially capture the sexual attentions of spectators. To judge from graffiti at Pompeii, some spectators lusted after Crescens. *Retiarii* were typically paired against the *murmillo* or *secutor*.

6. *Secutor, secutores*—"pursuer." The *secutores* seem to have risen to popularity in the middle part of the first century CE, and their armament is quite similar to the *murmillo*, although specifically designed to face the *retiarius*. As the typical opponent of the *retiarius*, another name for the *secutor* is the *contraretiarius*. As *retiarii* had to attack and retreat, the *secutor*'s tactic was to pursue aggressively. The primary difference between this type and the *murmillo* is that the *secutor*'s helmet has no brim or visor, but instead covers the whole face with two small holes for the eyes. The crest is small and finlike. These practical adjustments to the helmet made it more difficult for the *retiarius* to harm this gladiator with his trident or net, which could easily catch the crest of a *murmillo*'s helmet, although it must have been more difficult to see and to coordinate moves through this kind of helmet.

7. *Thraex, thraeces*—"Thracian." The Thracian gladiator type is one of the most popular in the imperial period, although it first appeared during the Republic. It is an ethnic type of gladiator, which means that the armament and equipment were meant to evoke a foreign people; in this case, it was the Thracian peoples, who lived in an area now largely occupied by northeastern Greece and Bulgaria. The Thracian gladiator also wore a loincloth and carried a small oblong shield and a short, curved sword (figure 4.5). He wore a brimmed helmet with a high crest that terminated in the form of a griffin. Other armament included high greaves that went to the thighs and armor strapped over his right arm, with which he wielded the sword. These gladiators were most often paired against the *hoplomachus* or *murmillo*. Titus's favorite gladiator type was the Thracian; he cheered for Thracians during the inaugural games and bantered with the crowd about their prowess.

Figure 4.5. A Roman terracotta oil lamp, from circa 50–100 CE, depicting a Thracian gladiator (Photograph © 2019, Museum of Fine Arts, Boston, Gift of Mrs. Orrin W. Mann, 49.407)

Although modern popular culture tends to conceive of gladiatorial combats always ending in death, most gladiators survived to fight multiple times. It was the *meridianum spectaculum* that offered wholesale death, and which was the bloodiest part of the day during games in the amphitheater. Gladiators, although slaves, were highly trained, skilled, and expensive to feed, lodge, and train. They also had some of the best medical care in the Roman world because of the amount of money invested in training these talented fighters. Galen was a famous Greek doctor who attended to gladiators in Pergamon in the second century CE and whose writings survive today. The crowd expected to see honorable and entertaining high-stakes combat between two highly skilled fighters, which need not always end in death. Death might come quickly from a lucky blow during combat or later from a wound received in combat. A particularly generous show sponsored by a *munerarius* might end in the deaths of several gladiators, although that would be expensive for the sponsor because he would have to pay extra fees to the gladiator school for their deaths. A gladiatorial fight typically continued until one of the participants raised his finger as a sign of submission. At that time, the *munerarius,* or the emperor in the Colosseum, would decide whether the defeated gladiator should live or die, usually after taking the pulse of the crowd's sentiments. If the crowd was convinced that he fought honorably and bravely, they would shout approval, and the sponsor would usually allow him to live. If, on the other hand, he was dishonorable or fought cowardly, the crowd might call for his death, pressuring the *munerarius* to order his execution there on the arena floor. If a gladiator's conduct was particularly offensive, his execution might be ordered to take place in the *spoliarium,* so that he did not receive the noble death on the arena floor.

The signal for the decision was *pollice verso,* which means "with a turned thumb." In modern popular culture and in Hollywood films, this has been portrayed as the "thumbs down" signal, although more probably it was the "thumbs up" signal, as in "put the sword in." Jean-Léon Gérôme's famous painting, *Pollice Verso*, shows a victorious *murmillo* standing over a defeated *retiarius* looking toward the emperor and the crowd for a signal. In the nineteenth-century mind, Gérôme conceived of the death signal as "thumbs down," as one sees an enthusiastic crowd, and a particularly bloodthirsty group of Vestal Virgins, signal for death with inverted thumbs (figure 4.6). In Gérôme's painting, under the defeated *retiarius* is a dead *murmillo* and, in the background, a dead *secutor.* A defeated gladiator who was granted reprieve received *missio* (discharge), meaning he survived the day and returned to the gladiator school. The "gladiator salute," an example of which is enacted in the movie *Gladiator* (2000) when the gladiators look at the emperor and say, "We who are about to die salute you," is another popular myth of the modern age. This saying is attested only during the reign of Claudius, when the emperor staged a naval battle on the Fucine Lake with ships manned by condemned prisoners; before combat they addressed the emperor this way.[48]

Although gladiators were not killed with the frequency portrayed by modern popular media, they faced significant risk; few lived long enough to win or earn their freedom from the arena. Gladiators who fought with particular valor

Figure 4.6. Jean-Léon Gérôme, *Pollice Verso* (Thumbs Down), 1872, oil on canvas (Collection of the Phoenix Art Museum, Museum purchase)

and skill might be freed by the sponsor after a combat. The freed gladiator was presented with a *rudis*, often mistranslated today as a wooden sword. It is also portrayed incorrectly in the film *Gladiator*, in which the character Proximo, a former gladiator who now owns a gladiator school, possesses a wooden sword given to him by the emperor Marcus Aurelius. The *rudis* was a rod, an implement carried by a *lanista*, and it symbolized freedom from service as a gladiator when presented to a gladiator.[49]

Several gladiator cemeteries are known to archaeologists, and many have been studied scientifically. At Ephesus, in modern Turkey, study of the bones from a gladiator cemetery tells us much about the lives and deaths of gladiators.[50] Remains of different gladiators showed evidence of broken bones that were professionally set and had healed; these were wounds received in combat that were attended to by highly skilled physicians. One skull had gouge marks over the eye that did not cause death and healed over; a *retiarius*'s trident undoubtedly inflicted these wounds. Some had evidence of healing after receiving blows from swords. Others had blunt-force trauma to the skull that caused death, suggesting a crushing blow from a shield received during combat or the death blow delivered when the *munerarius* ordered death at the end of a fight. The bones contained high levels of strontium, which can replace calcium in the bones. This suggests that the gladiators drank bone ash mixed with water and ate a diet heavy in barley and beans, which confirms what literary sources tell us about the diet of gladiators. They also had very enlarged muscle markers on their bones, attesting to the intense training conditions of the gladiator school.

Only two of Martial's epigrams in his *Book of Spectacles* describe gladiatorial combats under the Flavians. Both merit quotation. The first reads: "The fact that Mars the warrior serves you in invincible armour is not enough, Caesar; Venus herself serves as well."[51] This epigram alludes to fights between female gladiators in Flavian games in the Colosseum. We have already seen evidence for female *venatores* in these games; women too might occasionally fight as gladiators, although they were much rarer than male gladiators—hence, Martial's note of them as reflective of Caesar's remarkable games.[52] It is unclear how seriously the Roman crowd took female gladiators. They may have been presented as novelty and farce. In games of Domitian, Statius mentions them alongside midgets, suggesting the latter.[53] The second passage recounts a remarkable bout between two gladiators:

While Priscus continued to draw out the contest, and Verus likewise, and for a long time the struggle was evenly balanced on both sides, discharge was demanded for the stout fighters with loud and frequent shouting; but Caesar obeyed his own law (the law was that once the palm had been set up the fight had to proceed until a finger was raised): he did as he was allowed, making frequent awards of plate. Still, a resolution was found for the deadlocked contest: equal they fought, equal they yielded. To both Caesar awarded the wooden rod and the palm: thus courage and skill received their reward. This has happened under no emperor except you, Caesar. Two men fought and two men won.[54]

In this contest, both gladiators, Verus and Priscus, fought so long and bravely that the crowd asked the emperor to stop the fight, although the rules stated one must yield by raising a finger. The fight continued until, unbelievably, they happened to yield at the same time. The emperor, in an unprecedented display of munificence, then awarded both valiant gladiators palm branches, symbols of victory, and wooden rods freeing them from their lives as gladiators. We may assume that the crowd was thrilled with the emperor's display of generosity here—and, indeed, it might have egged him on. Suetonius mentions the expediency of listening to the crowd in his description of Titus's beneficence. He says that "at a gladiatorial show he declared that he would give it 'not after his own inclinations, but those of the spectators;' and what is more, he kept his word."[55]

Flooding the Colosseum for Naval Battles

One remarkable addition to games in the Colosseum was that in some of the earliest spectacles it was occasionally flooded for naval battles. Although ancient sources attest the flooding of the Colosseum, it has been a debated subject among scholars.[56] Cassius Dio, more than 100 years after the inaugural games, writes:

For Titus suddenly filled this same (amphi)theater with water and brought in horses and bulls and some other domesticated animals that had been taught to behave in the liquid element just as on land. He also brought in people on ships, who engaged in a sea-fight there, impersonating the Corcyreans and Corinthians; and others gave a similar exhibition outside the city in the grove of Gaius and Lucius, a place which Augustus had once excavated for this very purpose. There too, on the first day there was a gladiatorial exhibition and wild-beast hunt, the lake in front of the images having first been covered over with a platform of planks and wooden stands erected around it. On the second day there was a horse-race, and on the third day a naval battle between three thousand men, followed by an infantry battle. The "Athenians" conquered the "Syracusans" (these were the names the combatants used), made a landing on the islet and assaulted and captured a wall that had been constructed around the monument. These were the spectacles that were offered, and they continued for a hundred days.[57]

Here, Dio does not seem to be confused or conflating venues for the aquatic spectacles, for he clearly distinguishes between engagements Titus held in both the Colosseum and the Naumachia of Augustus. Suetonius, writing a couple of decades after Domitian's reign, claims that Domitian too flooded the Colosseum:

He constantly gave grand and costly entertainments, both in the amphitheatre and in the Circus, where in addition to the usual races between two-horse and four-horse chariots, he also exhibited two battles, one between forces of infantry and the other by horsemen; and he even gave a naval battle in the amphitheatre. . . . He often gave sea-fights almost with regular fleets, having dug a pool near the Tiber and surrounded it with seats; and he continued to witness the contests amid heavy rains.[58]

Suetonius's account of Domitian's naval spectacles is similar to Dio's treatment of Titus's, as both authors explicitly distinguish between the Colosseum and excavated basins near the Tiber River as venues for aquatic spectacles. The most difficult evidence to ignore is that of Martial, an eyewitness to the Flavian spectacles in the Colosseum about which he wrote. He also is clear about aquatic spectacles both in the Colosseum and in a purpose-built basin near the Tiber River. Regarding the Colosseum, he writes:

If you have arrived late from distant shores to watch this show, and this was your first day at the sacred spectacle, don't let the naval warfare deceive you with its craft, and the water that is just like the sea: here a short while ago was land. You don't believe it? Watch, while the waters wear Mars out. After a brief delay you will say "Here just now there was sea."[59]

This epigram must refer to the flooding of the Colosseum because Martial refers to water covering land and says there will soon be land again. The next three epigrams also refer to the flooding of the Colosseum. And Martial, like Cassius Dio, describes a separate naval battle that was held in the Naumachia of Augustus:

Here it was the labour of Augustus to pit fleets against one another and to rouse the waves with naval trumpet. What fraction of our Emperor's achievement does this amount to? Thetis and Galatea have seen strange beasts among the waves; Triton has seen chariots scorching in the watery dust, and thought his master's horses had galloped by; and while Nereus was organizing fierce battles for hostile fleets, he was awestruck at going on foot over limpid water. Whatever can be seen in both the circus and the amphitheater the lavish water has provided at a blast of Caesar's trumpet. Boasting about Fucinus and Trojan Nero's pools has to stop: posterity is to know just this one naval battle.[60]

There are reasons why the reality of the flooding of the Colosseum for naval combats has caused such controversy, despite the ancient testimony and Martial's own eyewitness account. First of all, we are accustomed to the Colosseum with its substructures in place, which would have precluded any aquatic spectacle there. Second, when discussing *naumachiae*, mock naval battles, we think of them as full-scale battles among large ships manned by condemned criminals (note that *naumachia* in Latin can refer to either the spectacle of a naval battle or the venue specially constructed for such spectacles). Such large-scale engagements required purpose-built excavated basins that were much larger than the Colosseum, such as the Naumachia of Augustus or the Naumachia of

Domitian. In her study of *naumachiae*, Coleman rightly points out that once the substructures of the Colosseum were installed at some point in Domitian's reign, it would have been impractical and virtually impossible to flood the arena, for it would have ruined the equipment below, and the *hypogeum* was not watertight.[61] Others have suggested that before the installation of the substructures there was a purpose-built basin for aquatic spectacles below the arena floor, although there is no archaeological evidence for it. Outside of Rome, some amphitheaters did have basins that supported aquatic spectacles.

In view of the incontrovertible literary attestations by Martial, Suetonius, and Cassius Dio, we must accept that the Colosseum was flooded for spectacles in its earliest games, although after the installation of the substructures at some point in Domitian's reign, aquatic displays in the Colosseum would not have been possible again. Mock naval battles in the Colosseum before the excavation of the *hypogeum* must have been scaled down immensely compared with the much larger-scale battles set in the purpose-built *naumachiae*. The arena floor of the Colosseum is large enough to accommodate two full-size warships, but it would have been impossible to bring them through the entrances, and the draft of such ships would have been too great for them to float in a flooded arena. Even if it had been technically possible, two large ships could hardly have maneuvered in the confined space. The naval battles in the Colosseum, then, must have been staged with significantly smaller ships. The purpose of flooding the amphitheater for a small-scale naval engagement was for the novelty and spectacle of it, as the arena would have been rapidly covered with water and then quickly restored to dry land after the spectacle. It was also an ideologically charged feat, casting the emperor as commanding power over nature. The first spectators in the Colosseum would have remembered that the Colosseum sat on the site of Nero's great lake, where he might also have held aquatic spectacles, and so the display might have alluded to that past while presenting exhibitions of the Flavian emperors that spectacularly surpassed anything that Nero had done. In the epigram cited earlier, Martial's invocation of "Fucinus and Trojan Nero's pools" invites readers to recall Claudius's great battle staged on the Fucine Lake and also Nero's *stagnum* and suggests that the Flavian emperor has surpassed both.

The Emperor, the Crowd, and Flavian Spectacles

The construction and dedication of the Colosseum and surrounding Flavian monuments communicated an important political ideology about the new dynasty, but the building also served the practical function of host to grand spectacles and, especially, gladiatorial combats. These bloody displays were no less political than the erection of the great amphitheater itself.

The first political and dynastic symbolism in the games would be the procession of images of the gods and deified emperors into the arena and their placement across from Titus on the first day of games in the new Colosseum. There, the Deified Augustus, the Deified Claudius, and the Deified Vespasian would have watched Titus's games, and all spectators would have seen the living emperor across from these gods, positioning him as their natural successor and as a future god himself.

The 100 days of games were unlike any Rome had witnessed before that time in terms of extent, diversity, and grandiosity. All this made for a lengthy display of the emperor's *munificentia* (lavish generosity) and power. Popular emperors arranged public spectacles in Rome; unpopular emperors did not. Tiberius notoriously neglected public entertainments to the degree that in 27 CE people from Rome traveled in great numbers to watch games at nearby Fidenae held in a shoddily erected wooden amphitheater that collapsed under the weight of spectators, killing thousands.[62] When Tiberius died, some sneered that his body should be burned in the amphitheater, so that at last he will have provided some entertainment.[63] Nonetheless, the Flavian emperors understood the popular appeal of games and could never be accused of neglecting their provision.

Exotic beasts were imported from the corners of the Roman Empire and beyond. In some of the earliest games in the Colosseum, Martial mentions a tiger from the Hyrcanian mountains, which lie in modern Iran; a host of North African beasts, such as lions, elephants, and a rhinoceros; and a bear from Caledonia (Scotland). Many Romans may never have seen such animals before, and their exhibition in the amphitheater communicated to the crowds the reach and power of the empire in which they lived and the superhuman qualities of their emperor to command such displays.

The midday executions punished those who broke the law. Staged as performances from myth, many of these executions enacted divine retribution on those who defied the gods. Such displays made their religious tales come alive in spectacular fashion. The amphitheater was an appropriate place for executions, since it was a uniquely Roman building with hierarchical seating arrangements that gave precedence to citizens typically exempted from such punishments. Those who died in the arena were noncitizens; they had subverted Roman order by resisting Rome or breaking the law, and they were justly punished in the Roman mind, just as others in myth were punished for their hubris against the gods. The amphitheater was strongly linked with the emperor and emperor worship. What better venue to punish those who broke Roman law and, by extension, had defied the emperor?

Similarly, gladiators were criminals or prisoners of war condemned to the gladiator school, or slaves sold to the school; they performed for the entertainment of Roman citizens. The collective viewing of spectacles in which animals, condemned criminals, and noncitizens fought and died for the amusement of the Romans reinforced a collective Roman identity, even while citizens were separated by class. Furthermore, the collective viewing of such spectacles communicated a Roman moral superiority, as the spectators enjoyed the entertainments and superior legal and class benefits their empire brought them in contrast with those performing and dying on the arena floor for their amusement.[64]

Throughout the *Book of Spectacles*, Martial ascribes the displays in the Colosseum to the power and generosity of the emperor. Frequently, the emperor is cast as a superhuman and godlike figure, exercising power over nature. This is why the emperor ordered the death of the performing lion after it mauled its trainer and why Martial claims Caesar's bull was carried aloft higher than Jupiter's. One epigram tells of a hunt in which dogs (Molossians) were chasing a deer in the arena when the doe suddenly stopped before the emperor, as if suppliant, and the dogs did not dare attack her there; for her deference to the emperor, the deer was spared.[65] Another epigram reads: "Respectful and suppliant, the elephant that was recently so formidable to a bull worships you, Caesar. It does not do this on command, nor on instruction from any trainer: believe me, it too feels the presence of our god."[66] Obviously, the elephant featured here was trained to kneel before the imperial box, although it was presented as a spontaneous act in which the crowd must have reveled, as it powerfully communicated the divinity of the emperor and his command exercised over nature itself. An elephant appears on gold and silver coins of Titus, contemporary with the 100 days of games (figure 4.7). Such a design immortalized the memory of Titus's games, and perhaps also the wondrous displays of deference that wild beasts, such as the elephant, performed before the emperor. The flooding of the amphitheater was also a display of imperial command over nature, as land was made wet and then quickly made dry again.

The games were also a place where the emperor could be seen expressing beneficence and mercy, as in the freeing of the deer. In the episode of Priscus and Verus, the emperor freed both gladiators for their amazing display of valor,

Figure 4.7. A gold coin (*aureus*) of Titus from 80 CE depicting on its obverse a portrait of Titus with his imperial titles. The reverse depicts an elephant. (Courtesy of the American Numismatic Society, 1944.100.41642)

much to the delight of the crowd. The crowd too enjoyed personal largess dispensed by the emperor. Cassius Dio recounts that in the Colosseum Titus would go to the upper levels and throw down wooden balls to the spectators. Throngs of citizens would clamor to catch these, for each was inscribed with a prize that they would receive upon taking it to a designated official.[67] Among the prizes, Dio lists some basic things, such as food items or an article of clothing, but he also records prizes that could amount to financial windfalls, if the balls were intercepted by citizens without much financial means: vessels of silver and gold, horses, pack animals, cattle, and slaves. The crowd saw the emperor enjoying the same sorts of entertainments they enjoyed and relished the generosity he lavished upon them. Suetonius says that Titus "refused nothing which anyone asked, and even urged them to ask for what they wished. Furthermore, he openly displayed his partiality for Thracian gladiators and bantered the people about it by words and gestures, always however preserving his dignity, as well as observing justice. Not to omit any act of condescension, he sometimes bathed in the baths which he had built, in company with the common people."[68] These public displays of generosity and personability portrayed him as an accessible man of the people. Even today, people enjoy seeing their political leaders at sporting events, enjoying the same games and expressing the same human qualities as the common people.

    Titus's 100 days of games, like the Flavian building program itself, linked him and his dynasty with the memories of the Deified Augustus and the Deified

Claudius, who both held remarkable spectacles and were concerned about the well-being of the people. The fact that Titus mounted displays in the Naumachia of Augustus during the 100 days of games makes this link apparent, as do later displays and the construction of a new *naumachia* in the reign of Domitian. If Titus's games were held for the consecration of Vespasian as a god, then it stands to reason that Domitian's first games in the amphitheater were held for Titus's consecration as a god. In such a scenario, during the games over which he first presided, Domitian sat across from images of the deified Julio-Claudians as well as his deified father and brother. Indeed, the coins of Domitian that depict the Colosseum unsubtly mark Titus's deification on the reverse, and Titus's name appears in the dative case, translating *"To the Deified Titus . . . ,"* perhaps referring to games in his honor (figure 2.12). In Titus's reign, the restoration coins and coins depicting the seats and divine attributes on the *pulvinar* were associated with coins marking Vespasian's deification, after a delay of some months; they provide evidence that the celebration of Vespasian's new status as a god in the Colosseum was the impetus behind the 100 days of games. Similarly, the *pulvinaria* coin types and the restoration coins continued into the first months of Domitian's reign and were struck alongside the Colosseum coins for the Deified Titus, also suggesting that Domitian celebrated his brother's deification with games there.

The Colosseum, the Flavian building program, and the games provided by the Flavian emperors all came together to communicate profound ideological and dynastic messages to the people of Rome, as the members of the Flavian dynasty were portrayed as worthy successors to the Julio-Claudians and as surpassing their achievements. The games were particularly lavish, but they were fleeting; the Colosseum would, however, endure. Art and literature of the Flavian era responded to the Colosseum and its earliest games, immortalizing the ephemeral.

-V-

The Colosseum and Its First Games in Flavian Art and Literature

CONSTRUCTION OF THE COLOSSEUM, and the Flavian building program more generally, boldly communicated the theme of military victory and dynastic aspirations modeled on Augustus, while hearkening back to the popular and practical sorts of buildings and programs undertaken by Claudius. The Flavian building program focused on the area of the Colosseum valley (the core of Nero's Domus Aurea) and, as an intended effect, diminished Nero's mark on the city while simultaneously promoting associations with the Deified Augustus and the Deified Claudius. The wondrous spectacles held by Titus and Domitian also recalled the feats of Augustus and Claudius, especially *naumachiae*, and eclipsed their exhibitions. Displays of emperor worship in the Colosseum, with the presence of the living emperor juxtaposed with images and attributes of the deified emperors, suggested the power and legitimacy of the living emperor. The Colosseum and surrounding Flavian monuments, built of stone and concrete, continued to stand as symbols of the new regime and what it represented, but their games were ephemeral. It is, therefore, worth surveying cultural reactions to the construction of the Colosseum and its first spectacles that are preserved in art and literature of the Flavian age.

Martial's *Book of Spectacles*

The *Book of Spectacles* is far more than a firsthand account of early games that took place either during Titus's inaugural games or in Domitian's reign. It is a work of panegyric, written in praise of the Flavian emperor for the lavish spectacles described therein.[1] Throughout, the emperor is addressed as the agent behind the spectacles and the reason for marvelous wonders that the crowd witnesses in the unprecedented games. The preceding chapter noted that a common theme in the *Book of Spectacles* is the emperor's power over nature, either by command and ingenuity, such as the flooding of the amphitheater, or by the spontaneous deference of the animal kingdom before the emperor—for example, the submission of the doe that stopped, as if suppliant, before the emperor as hunting dogs pursued her or the trained elephant that knelt before the emperor.

The theme of imperial command over nature is one that sometimes leads scholars to attribute the *Book of Spectacles* to the reign of Domitian rather than to Titus, because power over nature is a recurrent theme in literature produced in Domitian's reign. In Martial's *Epigrams*, some books of which were written in praise of Domitian, the theme also comes up in relation to his spectacles, as in a display of lions hunting hares in which the lions, instead of killing them, gingerly played with them; Martial compares Domitian's exhibition of the lions with Jupiter who, as an eagle, abducted the desirable youth Ganymede and did not harm the boy's flesh with his talons.[2] The language used in the epigram with the kneeling elephant that "too feels our god" (*nostrum sentit et ille deum*) has also been one reason to ascribe the *Book of Spectacles* to Domitian's reign, for it is well known that he was often addressed as *Dominus et Deus*, "master and god," and at his command according to Suetonius and Cassius Dio.[3] Brian W. Jones has cogently argued, however, that flatterers used such a form of address to Domitian and that the idea that Domitian insisted upon it derives from post-Domitianic literature that vilified Domitian, just as post-Neronian literature maligned Nero.[4]

As Coleman points out, the language of divinity in the *Book of Spectacles* is insufficient evidence to associate it with Domitian, for other poets and panegyrists similarly addressed emperors as such, and Martial might well have addressed Titus as "our god" too.[5] One must also keep in mind that the living emperor himself was presented as a semidivine figure, seated across from images of the gods and the deified emperor. The act of the elephant appearing to worship the emperor would rightly prompt the use of the word in such a context.

The theme of imperial power over nature is by no means unique to Domitian's reign and is widely portrayed in art, building, and literature in both earlier and later periods of imperial history.[6] The spectacular character of the games also provided an opportunity for the emperor to display positive virtues such as generosity and mercy, for which Martial praised him. The emperor granted clemency to the supplicant deer and freedom to the valiant gladiators, Priscus and Verus.

Martial also recounts that marvels in the arena occurred because of the emperor's superhuman presence, such as the sow that miraculously gave birth when struck by a hunting spear or the remarkable displays of the rare rhinoceros. Martial's mention of Nero's pools and the Fucine Lake, where Claudius had staged a naval battle, is meant to suggest that aquatic spectacles mounted by the Flavian emperor were greater than anything that had been achieved before in the provision of games in the city of Rome. The terrestrial displays commanded by the emperor are similarly praised for surpassing anything that came before, even in myth. Female hunters and gladiators appeared in the games, ascribed to the novelty of the emperor's spectacles; the deeds of the animal fighter, Carpophorus, are said to have exceeded the feats of Hercules, and Caesar's bull was carried higher aloft than Jupiter's.

Martial also praises the emperor for the magnificence of the venue itself. The first epigram in the *Book of Spectacles* begins by invoking several Wonders of the World that were built in foreign lands prior to Roman conquest: the Pyramids at Giza, the Hanging Gardens of Babylon, the Temple of Artemis at Ephesus, the Altar of Horn at Delos, and the Mausoleum at Halicarnassus. It concludes: "All labour yields to Caesar's amphitheatre: Fame will tell of one work instead of them all."[7] The scale and complexity of the building were such that the Romans might well have conceived of this new amphitheater as something that competed with and surpassed the Seven Wonders of the Ancient World, as Martial says quite plainly here about the new amphitheater.

The next two epigrams are related in their focus on the building. Martial's second epigram (quoted in chapter 1) describes the Colosseum and Flavian building in the area as a response to Nero and presents the Flavian emperor as a restorer of Rome. In the third epigram, Martial takes us inside the amphitheater and harps upon the international diversity of the spectators. He claims that there is no nation so barbarous or remote that it does not have a representative from it at these games. He goes on to name specific groups of foreign peoples represented among the crowd: Thracians, from what is essentially modern Bulgaria; the Sarmatians, a nomadic people who settled on the Danube

River; a people who drink from the source of the Nile River beyond Egypt; a people from the British Isles; Arabs; the Sabaei, from what is modern Yemen; Cilicians, who lived on the southern coast of Asia Minor (modern Turkey); the Sugambri, a Germanic tribe that lived along the Rhine River; and Ethiopians. He concludes the epigram: "The speech of the peoples sounds different and yet, when you are hailed as the true father of the fatherland, they all then speak as one."[8] People from the corners of the Roman Empire and beyond have come to witness games in this newest Wonder of the World, Martial alleges, although we must expect there is some exaggeration here. These epigrams are, after all, a work of panegyric to flatter the emperor, and this one in particular is meant to convey the vastness and diversity of the empire itself, over which the emperor rules. We are told that despite the differences among the tongues, all saluted the emperor as *pater patriae*, father of the fatherland, to pay homage to the emperor and his benefaction.

Just as the Flavian emperors through their policies and building programs cultivated associations and ideological links with Augustus and Claudius, a literate audience would have also recognized in Martial's poems intertextual allusions to literature produced during the reigns of past emperors and under their patronage. For instance, Martial's presentation of the Colosseum after listing some Wonders of the World draws upon the "marvels-of-the-city" theme deployed by poets in the age of Augustus. Additionally, Martial's claim that foreign races from the far-flung corners of the empire came to hail the emperor as *pater patriae* is based on the literary prototype of the *Res Gestae Divi Augusti* (The Achievements of the Divine Augustus), a text authored by Augustus and inscribed on bronze columns outside of his mausoleum when he died. Augustus concluded his *Res Gestae* with his receipt of the title *pater patriae* after having named 55 provinces, lands, peoples, cities, and bodies of water earlier in the text.[9] So, in addition to the overt praise directed toward the emperor in the *Book of Spectacles*, recording his unprecedented games, there is thus another layer to the panegyric as Martial aligned himself and his work with poets of former ages, promoting his own literary status and recognizing that the Flavians were, indeed, ushering in something of a new Augustan age, complementing their actions and ideological strategy.

The Colosseum and Its Games in Flavian Coinage and Art

The coinage of imperial Rome typically bears the portrait of the reigning emperor on one side and some other ideologically charged design on the other.

Images on Roman imperial coins were always changing and topical. Modern Western coins are, by comparison, monotonous in terms of the images they represent and the messages they carry. Images do not change frequently on the coins, and the topics they relate to are seldom current. In Titus's 27-month reign, dozens of distinct images appeared on the reverses of his coins, which is a significantly greater variety than what one would, until recently, typically witness on the coins in modern America or Europe over the course of a few decades. Images on Roman coins were also topical, relating to recent events, such as public building, military victories, festivals, and qualities ascribed to the emperor.

Designs on the imperial coinage are often said to be a form of propaganda that was concocted by the emperor or some close adviser to communicate the regime's hegemony and political agenda or to remind people of the benefits brought by the regime to justify its claim to power. Nevertheless, there is an alternative way of looking at the coinage. Their images often have much in common with contemporary panegyric and praise of the emperor, and there are reasons to attribute the agency behind the formulation and choice of the designs to senatorial or equestrian officials overseeing operations in the mint; if the images are a form of visual praise, the emperor would be among the audiences of the designs on the coins.[10] Not only does the interpretation explain parallels between the imagery and contemporary poetry and panegyric, but it also fits into the broader Roman culture of praise, as in the erection of honorary monuments, such as triumphal arches, dedicated to the emperor in praise of and thanks for his actions and his achievements. Indeed, the scholarly interpretation of Roman art and architecture more generally has avoided the notion of top-down propaganda and notes panegyrical qualities in relief sculptures and other visual media.[11] As many Flavian coins referred to the Colosseum's construction and its games, it is worth considering whether these were the product of top-down propaganda or of panegyric in the vein of Martial's *Book of Spectacles*.

Traditionally, the Colosseum coins of Titus and of Domitian for the Deified Titus (figure 2.12) are interpreted as communicating Flavian legitimacy and advertising the construction of the amphitheater and the first spectacles there, not dissimilar to the "propaganda" model just outlined. Although there are variants of the Colosseum coins that depict the amphitheater with the Meta Sudans and the *porticus* of the Baths of Titus on opposite sides of it, or lacking them altogether, most extant specimens struck under Titus, and all struck under Domitian, show the amphitheater with the Meta Sudans to the Colosseum's left and the *porticus* of the Baths of Titus to its right.[12] This arrangement of the flanking monuments provides a view of the southern façade of the amphitheater and can be achieved only from the area of the terrace of the Temple of the Deified Claudius (compare with figure 2.3). The vantage point from which public buildings were depicted could have significance, for Coleman has observed that the depiction of the Circus Maximus on coins of Trajan, where it is viewed from the direction of the Palatine Hill, could refer to imperial patronage because the emperor lived there; the vantage point also highlighted the solar associations of the Circus Maximus, as the Temple of the Sun built into the seating of the Circus Maximus and the obelisk at its center are visible, and the Palatine was home to the Temple of Apollo.[13]

On the Colosseum coins, the view of the Colosseum and associated Flavian monuments from the area of the Temple of the Deified Claudius seems to cohere remarkably well with the second epigram in Martial's *Book of Spectacles* (quoted in chapter 1). Describing Flavian construction in the area of the Colosseum, which replaced important parts of Nero's Domus Aurea, Martial explicitly mentions the Colosseum, the Baths of Titus, a "lofty framework that rises in the middle of the road" (perhaps the Arch of Titus under construction), and the Claudian *porticus* spreading shade onto the area.[14] The Claudian *porticus* must be a reference to the completion of the Temple of the Deified Claudius by Vespasian. What the epigram and the coins have in common is the depiction of the amphitheater and adjacent Flavian buildings; both specifically call attention to the Baths of Titus. The coins also depict the Meta Sudans, which made strong ideological links with Augustus. As Martial refers to the Temple of the Deified Claudius, the coins depicting the Colosseum valley from the vantage point of the Temple of the Deified Claudius also make a similar link with that emperor. The reverses of the Flavian Colosseum coins show Titus seated triumphantly on a curule chair among the arms captured from the Jewish Revolt and holding a branch, symbolizing peace. This overt reference to Flavian victory in the Jewish Revolt reminds viewers that the construction of the Colosseum was financed with the spoils of the war, as was also indicated on the dedicatory inscription and elements of the sculptural details depicted on the Colosseum's façade on the other side. The only visual prototype on Roman coins for such an unusual representation of the emperor is found on coins of Claudius that depict him seated the same way, among the arms captured during his invasion of Britain (figure 3.7). Coins of Claudius were still in circulation during the reigns of Titus and Domitian, and so the similarities in their portrayal would have invited comparison between the military achievements of Titus and Claudius.

Visual allusions to the Deified Augustus and the Deified Claudius on the Colosseum coins presented Titus as a legitimate ruler following their positive models. While the policies, actions, and building programs of Vespasian, Titus, and Domitian cultivated ideological associations with these two Julio-Claudian emperors, this imagery and its message need not necessarily have been formulated by the emperor but, instead, may have been concocted to praise him, for others had projected Augustus and Claudius onto the identity of the Flavian emperor. The *Lex de Imperio Vespasiani*, a decree of the Senate investing powers first held by Augustus onto Vespasian, invoked the name of Claudius as a precedent. Martial's epigrams in the *Book of Spectacles* drew upon Augustan prototypes and modes of praise, and Silius Italicus praised the Flavians as successors to the deified Julio-Claudian emperors: "Later still, godlike excellence shall come from Cures and soar to heaven; and a warrior family, reared on the berry that grows in the Sabine land, shall increase the fame of the Julii."[15] In the reign of Hadrian, Suetonius projected Augustus onto Titus in his *Deified Titus*.[16]

It is also worth observing that the Colosseum coins of Domitian, struck for the Deified Titus, bear an accompanying text that appears in the dative case, translating "*To* the Deified Titus." This suggests not only games for the Deified Titus in the Colosseum but also praise directed toward the Deified Titus. The panegyrical sense might be heightened by the letters "S[ENATVS] C[ONSVLTO]" on the bronze coinage—that is, "by decree of the Senate"—which could be a mark of senatorial agency in honors bestowed upon the emperors, although the significance of "S C" is a debated topic.

The restoration coins of Titus and Domitian that revived coin designs of past emperors, together with other coins referring to the gods and deified emperors on the *pulvinar* (e.g., figures 2.22–2.23) and the coins celebrating the elevation of Vespasian as a deified emperor, can also be interpreted as part of a broader visual program of praise directed at the Flavian emperors at the time when the ideologically laden amphitheater was finally inaugurated. The continuation of the same imagery early into Domitian's reign transferred visual praise directed toward the Deified Vespasian and to Titus to honors directed toward the Deified Titus and to Domitian.

It is also possible to see a parallel between Martial's praise of the emperors and coins of Titus that depict an elephant (figure 4.7). While the elephant may have been emblematic of the extravagant inaugural games, in which elephants participated in fights with other animals, Martial also remarked upon the kneeling elephant that must have awed the crowds as it recognized the emperor and offered deference to him. The image of the elephant would have reminded any who were at the games not only of the spectacles involving the elephants but also of the spontaneous and wondrous deference of the elephant, if indeed this event took place under Titus rather than under Domitian. The elephant also had some religious significance and was associated with the emperor, for elephants were connected with the cults of Dionysus and Alexander the Great, and the emperor owned a herd of elephants in Rome. Coleman interprets the significance of the kneeling elephant then as an unsubtle allusion to the emperor's divinity.[17] The elephant on the coins could also be a form of visual praise directed toward the emperor, exalting his dominion over nature itself and his superhuman status.

Coins of Domitian that depict a rhinoceros recalled the entertaining fights involving the rhinoceros that Martial recounts and the emperor's responsibility for those events (figure 4.2). Similar to the epigrams addressed to the emperor describing the spectacles involving the elephant, the image of the rhinoceros did not serve as a propagandistic reminder of the exhibition of a rhinoceros but echoed the sort of praise that Martial wrote.

Other coins that referred to games in later periods of Roman history have parallels with written praise. For instance, coins struck between 202 and 209 CE, during the reign of Septimius Severus, depict the central barrier of the Circus Maximus outfitted in the form of a ship, with a hull around it and the obelisk acting as its mast. Surrounding it are animals and the accompanying text "LAETITIA TEMPORVM" (the happiness of the times). Cassius Dio, who witnessed the event and described it in praise of the emperor, recounts this spectacle.[18] In this exhibition in the Circus Maximus, the barrier was rigged like a ship and staged to fall apart to release various animals for a *venatio*. Dio's description is also very similar to an honorary inscription that was dedicated to Septimius Severus and that used language very similar to "LAETITIA TEMPORVM." This suggests that the designer of the image drew upon contemporary praise directed toward the emperor for this spectacle.[19]

After the end of the Flavian dynasty, images of the Colosseum were struck on coins under two later emperors.[20] The first instance occurred on coins struck for Severus Alexander. These were clearly modeled on Flavian representations, since the Colosseum is flanked by other monuments and from a perspective that allows both the façade and part of the *cavea* to be seen. The flanking monuments on the gold coins cannot be identified definitively, but to the left of the amphitheater is a figure within an arch. On the bronze and copper coins, there are three figures to the left of the amphitheater and next to the Meta Sudans; to the Colosseum's right is a two-story *porticus*, which must be the Baths of Titus. Inside the amphitheater, a gladiatorial combat takes place on the arena floor. The inclusion of the figures next to the amphitheater may suggest their involvement in some sort of rededication ceremony, for the occasion for the striking of these coins was Severus Alexander's reconstruction after the fire of 217 CE. The Baths of Titus were also damaged in that fire, which makes the reappearance of the *porticus* of the Baths of Titus on the coins significant. After Severus Alexander's death in 235 CE, Gordian III (241–244 CE) struck medallions depicting the Colosseum flanked by the Colossus of Sol on the left, with the Meta Sudans in front of it, and the *porticus* of the Baths of Titus on the right, similar to the Flavian coins (figure 5.1). Inside the amphitheater is a fight between an elephant and a bull, recalling a similar exhibition under the Flavians described by Martial, and a large representation of the emperor seated among the crowd. The occasion for the production of these medallions was probably further restorations on the Colosseum, since another source suggests that work was still needed on the Colosseum and the Baths of Titus, even after Severus Alexander's death.[21]

In addition to Flavian coins that refer to the Colosseum and its earliest spectacles, a section of the frieze from the Temple of the Deified Vespasian and

Figure 5.1. A bronze medallion of Gordian III from circa 241–244 CE. The obverse depicts a portrait of the emperor in armor and his imperial titles; the reverse depicts the Colosseum flanked by the Meta Sudans and the Colossus of Sol on the left and the *porticus* of the Baths of Titus on the right. On the arena floor, a fight between an elephant and a bull takes place. (© Trustees of the British Museum)

Titus in the Forum Romanum appears to recall specific events described in Martial's *Book of Spectacles*. Work on the temple for the Deified Vespasian began in the reign of Titus but was completed in the reign of Domitian after Titus passed away.[22] The section of the frieze in question depicts ritual implements and, most importantly, a vessel with two registers (figure 5.2). The upper register on the vessel shows a man spearing a very large lion, and the lower register shows a rhinoceros fighting a bull. Both of these events are recorded by Martial, who speaks of Carpophorus felling a large lion and the rhinoceros tossing a bull. As the *Book of Spectacles* praised the Flavian emperor for the wondrous spectacles

Figure 5.2. A section of the frieze of the Temple of the Deified Vespasian and Titus depicting a vessel with scenes related to Martial's *Book of Spectacles*. The upper register on the vessel shows a man (Carpophorus?) spearing a lion; the lower register shows a rhinoceros fighting a bull. (Musei Capitolini, Rome. Photograph: Nathan T. Elkins, 2017)

offered in his arena, we seem to have a visualization of that praise carved in stone on the temple.[23] The panegyrical character of the image may be emphasized further by attention to the temple's dedicatory inscription, which reads "DIVO VESPASIANO AVGVSTO SPQR" (The Senate and Roman People *to* the Deified Vespasian Augustus).[24] The use of the dative case in the dedication to the Deified Vespasian, with the Senate and Roman People as the dedicants, is similar to the use of the dative on the Colosseum coins of Domitian for the Deified Titus (figure 2.12). The inscription records only a dedication to Vespasian, although later sources, the Chronographer of 354 CE and the *Regionaries*, refer to it as the Temple of the Deified Vespasian and Titus, and it is logical that both were worshipped here after Titus's death.

The inauguration of the Colosseum in 80 CE and Titus's 100 days of games were the most significant events of that emperor's reign. Not only were those events themselves of great importance, but they signaled a climax in the Flavian ideological program that had been initiated as soon as Vespasian seized imperial power and set about promoting his legitimacy and dynastic ambitions. The year 80 CE saw the culmination of Vespasian's agenda through the inauguration of his amphitheater, the chief component of his building program, which also strongly linked him and his family with Augustus's and Claudius's memory and their military achievements. The same year witnessed Vespasian's deification, which was probably also the rationale for the 100 days of games over which Titus presided, and which also signaled the fulfillment of Flavian dynastic ambitions through his successful apotheosis, for he was the first non-Julio-Claudian emperor to be deified.

The games organized by Domitian in the Colosseum also were politically charged, as he continued to promote in his policies and building program the same ideologies that Vespasian and Titus had advanced, and he would have presided over games celebrating Titus's deification, adding further legitimacy to his own rule. Domitian was also strongly associated with the construction of the amphitheater, having completed the Colosseum's attic level and installing the *hypogeum*. Authors of the day dedicated poems of thanksgiving and praise to the Flavian emperors for their games and the generous gift of the Colosseum and, more generally, for their restoration of the city after Nero's fall. That praise, as well as the significance of 80 CE and thereafter, was also immortalized in art and coinage, which have much in common with Martial's *Book of Spectacles*.

EPILOGUE

The End of the "Flavian" Amphitheater

ON THE LAST DAY of his 100 days of games, Titus was sad to see it all end, and he wept bitterly before the crowd.[1] His depression soon worsened, because an animal had escaped him during a sacrifice, a very bad portent. In the following year, he set out for his ancestral homeland in the Sabine Hills, became ill, and eventually died in the same house in which his father, Vespasian, had died two years before. The inaugural games over which Titus presided were staged to celebrate Vespasian as the newest deified emperor. Just as Titus had died in the same house as his father had, his deification was celebrated in the same amphitheater as his father's had been, during the first games over which Domitian officiated.

Why did Titus weep so bitterly at the conclusion of his games? We can only speculate. Perhaps he felt something was wrong and knew that his life would soon come to an end; perhaps he wept for his father who had not lived long enough to inaugurate the amphitheater together with him and his brother; or, perhaps, he knew that the dedication of the amphitheater and the 100 days of spectacles would be the greatest achievements of his reign and it was all over. Whatever the case may be, we may observe that what Vespasian initiated, what Titus inaugurated, and what Domitian finished was distinctly Flavian. The actions of these emperors aligned them with the "good" Julio-Claudian emperors to portray them as worthy successors, and the focus of their building program and the placement of the Colosseum dismantled Nero's Domus Aurea to present them as restorers of Rome. The construction of the Colosseum and other monuments in the area recalled the Deified Augustus and the Deified

Claudius in multiple ways and symbolized Flavian distinction and victory in warfare. The games staged in the Colosseum further connected the new dynasty with the old through the display of images of the deified emperors and also through the religious impetus behind the games themselves. The lavish spectacles communicated to the crowds the superhuman qualities of their emperor, emphasized the breadth of the empire over which he reigned, and provided an opportunity for his subjects to see him dispensing positive virtues such as mercy and generosity. The great significance of the Colosseum's completion and the wonder of the first spectacles held there is indicated by contemporary praise directed toward the emperor in literature, coinage, and art.

Nevertheless, in 96 CE, Domitian was assassinated, his memory was damned, and a new regime took power. The Colosseum would continue to be used for magnificent spectacles offered by subsequent emperors and dynasties that rose and fell as the generations passed, but the Flavian Amphitheater was Flavian no more. As time passed, the historical events that charged the Colosseum and its first spectacles with deep political and dynastic meaning were no longer relevant, especially as memories faded and the generations who remembered Vespasian, Titus, and Domitian, and the circumstances that brought them to power, died off. The monument itself simply became the locus for gladiatorial combats and associated spectacles in Rome.

We observe shifts in the meaning and resonance of monuments and events in our own world today. The Olympic Stadium (Olympiastadion) in Berlin was completed in 1936 during the rule of the Third Reich. Hitler ordered its construction and had intended it to be a marvelous stage to display his nation's racial superiority in the 1936 Summer Olympics. The stadium was part of a bigger complex and it was outfitted with the ostentatious emblems of the Nazi regime. These symbols were stripped from the building after the conclusion of World War II, although the stadium remained and has undergone subsequent renovations. Now, it is a multipurpose sporting arena, often host to international soccer matches. Few spectators think of the original propagandistic function of the building when they go to the stadium today, as it no longer serves the myriad ideological functions it once did for a now vanquished regime.

Another example of shifting resonances through the passage of time may be observed in the Vietnam Veterans Memorial in Washington, DC, which was completed in 1982. At the time of its realization, the memorial was an emotionally charged monument with nearly 58,000 names of American casualties on the polished granite surface of the wall. The first visitors displayed raw emotions when it was set up less than a decade after the controversial war ended, for it touched that generation the most. Those first visitors had recently lost spouses, siblings, children, or grandchildren to the war. Today, many who visit the site were very young, or not yet born, when it was built and may have only a surviving parent, grandparent, or another older relative who was in the war. Without having lived during the war or knowing people who died in it, their emotional connection is lesser than their parents or grandparents. Within the next few decades, the generation for whom this monument was most poignant will be gone and it will become a historical relic of the American past. Similarly, college students now do not remember the attacks on September 11, 2001, and will not relate to or understand the emotional impact of the event or the subsequent memorial monuments in quite the same way as those of us who watched it on television that morning in our own college dorm rooms, or who experienced the terror and sorrow firsthand in New York and Washington, DC, that day, or who had loved ones who died in the towers, the Pentagon, or in the airplane crash in Pennsylvania. Buildings and monuments have specific and profound political and/or emotional resonances associated with certain times and places. Although the Colosseum and its Flavian games bore ideological significance for the Flavian regime, that significance quickly faded after the deaths of Titus and Domitian.

After Flavian Rome, the Colosseum took on new meanings and functions, as it became a fixture from an old dynasty. It continued to be the primary venue for amphitheater games in Rome through the later empire when gladiatorial combats and animal spectacles gradually decreased in frequency and ultimately vanished. The last recorded gladiatorial fight in the Colosseum was during the reign of Honorius in 404 CE and the last recorded *venatio* in Rome took place in 523 CE. Outside of Rome, evidence suggests that gladiatorial combats ceased to take place in the Roman Empire after the middle of the fifth century CE and that animal hunts ended around the middle of the sixth century CE. During the last recorded gladiatorial combat in the Colosseum, it is said that a Christian monk attempted to stop the fight and that the crowd killed him for intervening. That episode led to Honorius's ban on gladiatorial combats at Rome.

Indeed, it is often assumed that the rise of Christianity directly led to the extinction of violent spectacles, such as animal hunts and gladiatorial combats. The historical reality is, however, much more complex.[2] Even before Christianity became a majority religion in the empire in the fourth century CE, these sorts of spectacles had been declining already in both frequency and extravagance. Economic conditions in the third and fourth centuries impaired the ability to hold expensive games. Animals perished less frequently in *venationes* in the later Roman Empire, as emphasis shifted to exhibitions of performing and trained animals, which allowed them to appear at multiple shows that were cheaper to produce. Congruent with the economic difficulties were changing cultural modes of public benefaction. In the periods of the Republic and early Roman Empire, wealthy citizens expended excess wealth on public monuments and lavish games; in the later Roman Empire, they gave to public welfare programs and for the enhancement of church communities. Independently of Christianity, some Roman authors had voiced philosophical opposition to violent games centuries before Christianity even took root.

Animal spectacles, public executions, and gladiatorial combats continued to be held during the reigns of the Christian emperors, who first came to power in the early fourth century CE. Many early Christian writers did not condemn the violence inherent in the games as much as they abhorred the relationship of those games and amphitheaters with the worship of the gods and emperors. The Colosseum continued to be used as a venue for brutal public executions into the early Middle Ages, and under Christian authority. Under Pope Stephen III (768–772 CE), the eyes and tongue of a criminal were publicly ripped out in the arena.

What had been a complex monument of dynastic ideology for the Flavian emperors became a monument to death in the Middle Ages. After the fall of the Roman Empire and the end of traditional amphitheater games, medieval Christians saw the Colosseum as a symbol of Christian martyrdom, believing it to be a place where Christians died for their faith during periods of cruel Roman persecution.[3] The idea that the Colosseum saw Christians executed for their faith is still a common belief. Nonetheless, this is Christian mythology. First, the frequency and severity of Roman persecution of Christians have been overstated. In fact, the Romans in general were more tolerant of other religions than Christian authorities were. Beginning in the fourth century CE, the rule of Christian emperors saw progressively more legislation aimed at restricting and eradicating other religions, including limitations placed on the practice of Judaism. Theodosius (379–395 CE) decreed the state religion to be Christianity, and he issued bans on sacrifice, auspices (taking omens from watching the flights of birds), and the general practice of the traditional Roman state religion and of other religions that had competed with Christianity during the period of its rise. He ordered the temples closed, at which time many were vandalized, destroyed, or turned into churches, and followers of the old religions often faced persecution, violence, and death.

Roman persecutions of Christianity in the first two centuries CE were periodic and localized, not prosecuted throughout the Roman Empire and not sustained. Before Christianity's rise to prominence, Roman authorities had generally allowed the practice of foreign religions, so long as followers of that religion recognized Roman political authority and paid taxes. The polytheistic mind accepted that other gods existed, whether one worshipped those gods or not, whereas the monotheistic Christian mind denied the existence of any other divinity. It is thus informative that on occasions when Christians were tried before the Roman courts, the crime for which they were often prosecuted was atheism, because their unwillingness to recognize other divinities was strange and upset the Roman concept of *pax deorum* (peace of the gods). In Roman thought, disturbing the *pax deorum* could cause great calamities, upheaval, and disrupt peace on earth itself, as the gods were angered. Examples of a rather tolerant attitude on behalf of authorities in the early Roman Empire may be observed in the correspondence between Pliny the Younger, the governor of Bithynia and Pontus (on the northern coast of modern Turkey), and the emperor Trajan in the early second century CE.[4] Trajan instructed Pliny not to search out Christians and to give them several opportunities on trial to say what needed to be said to escape penalties if they were brought before the courts. Although the first state-sanctioned persecution of Christians is popularly believed to have taken place under Nero, as Christians were blamed for the Great Fire of 64 CE according to Tacitus, there is no evidence for either a wholesale persecution of Christians or a targeting of them as a specific group in the empire in the aftermath of the fire.[5] In fact, Christians could be quite open in the practice of their religion in the Roman Empire. At Dura-Europos, in modern Syria, a Christian house-church with overt Christian decoration opened onto a public street and was among several religious buildings that the city hosted, including temples to Graeco-Roman gods, Persian gods, and a Jewish synagogue. All of this is suggestive of the religious diversity and apparent coexistence of religions in this Roman city.

In the third century CE, things started to get more challenging for the increasing number of Christians in the empire, as recognition of Roman political authority involved acknowledgments of the emperor's divinity through public sacrifice. Jews were exempted from this, as their leaders negotiated for it; on the other hand, Christians did not have the long historical precedence of the Jewish religion, which the Romans respected, and their leaders did not seek exemptions. Instead, some Christians flaunted their refusal to participate and actively turned themselves over to Roman authorities for punishment. They believed that suffering the humiliation and brutality of public execution would guarantee their place in heaven and would win converts to the faith. The search for a gruesome public martyrdom became so prevalent among some Christians that Roman authorities began to dismiss them or to execute them in private, robbing them of their desired deaths, while Christian authorities denounced the practice of actively seeking martyrdom. There really was no state-led persecution of Christians until the reign of Trajan Decius, who instigated one in 250 CE. On occasions when Christians were put to death in the arena, it was not necessarily because they were Christian but because they broke Roman law, and their mode of punishment was the same as for other condemned criminals.

Finally, although Christians were executed in some of the provincial amphitheaters, as at Lugdunum and Carthage, there is no evidence for the execution of Christians in the Colosseum. The Colosseum was not in operation at the time of any of the persecutions in Rome. Executions of Christians in Rome during periods of persecution would have taken place in the Circus of Gaius and Nero, where Peter was executed, or in the Circus Maximus, which is today an open park where families often walk their dogs. The Circus Maximus was never popularly recognized as a place of Christian martyrdom, and so it did not receive the same protections and attention after the fall of the Roman Empire. By the nineteenth century, modern industrial buildings sat on the site of the Circus Maximus.

Although the idea that the Colosseum was a place of Christian martyrdom under a hostile imperial government is fallacious, it saved the building from dilapidation, as the popes protected it because of its perceived holy significance. In the seventeenth century, during the papacy of Pope Innocent XI (1656–1689), the Church approached the architect and sculptor Gian Lorenzo Bernini with a plan to build a church to the Christian martyrs in the Colosseum, but he refused, suggesting that the ruins should stand as they are. The architect Carlo Fontana then pursued the project, but it never materialized. Pope Benedict XIV (1740–1758) set up the Stations of the Cross around the Colosseum, urged to do so by Leonard of Port Maurice. He also forbade the use of the Colosseum as a quarry for building material, as it was a sacred monument to the Christian martyrs. Pope Pius IX (1846–1878) struck a medal in 1851 referring to the Stations of the Cross at the holy site of the Colosseum; that pope also ordered further preservation work in 1852 to avoid collapse of the vaults. An inscription adjacent to the modern buttresses records his work and refers to previous popes and the Stations of the Cross (figure 2.1). Another inscription of Pope Pius IX appears today over the northern entrance on the short axis of the Colosseum, the entrance that the emperor used (figure 2.10). Today, the Stations of the Cross are still said by the pope at the Colosseum. The Christian belief that the Colosseum was a sacred site, and the consequent papal stewardship of it, ultimately deterred people from robbing out more stones and clamps from the monument, allowing for major preservation efforts in the eighteenth and nineteenth centuries.

The Colosseum, today, is one of Europe's biggest tourist attractions, which creates some challenges for the preservation of the site. Unfortunately, some tourists abscond with bricks and stones pried out of passageways, or deface the monument with graffiti, actively contributing to the destruction of the amphitheater. In light of its continuing status as an icon, we might pose the question: "What does the Colosseum mean to us now, in the twenty-first century, and why is it a monument worth preserving, studying, and teaching?" To an historian of ancient Rome, the Colosseum is the place for countless colorful episodes in Roman history, the site of extravagant and bloody games, an architectural and engineering marvel, and a building laden with ideological symbolism and significance for the emperors who built it and for the crowds who watched spectacles there. Historians aim to study the past on its own terms, in the historical, political, and cultural contexts of the time. The historian's commitment is to be objective. Nevertheless, history is not simply confined to understanding the past. Although most students who study history, archaeology, or classical studies will not necessarily enter those fields, their value—and the value of the humanities more broadly—is essential and cannot be overstated. Students of the past learn to think critically through the close examination of a specific time and place within particular cultural, political, and social contexts, thereby gaining insight into the complexities of the human condition and the workings of civilization itself. That development of critical-thought processes allows one to apply historical lessons to today, or at least to think more deeply about the contemporary world. That thought is multidimensional, about cause, effect, implication, and nuance, and it considers the ramifications or potential eventualities of ideas, policies, statements, and actions. The Colosseum, then, is not a dead relic from the past, for our knowledge of the past can be a mirror held up to the present if we allow ourselves the opportunity for introspection and reflection.

People have a natural tendency to look back on the past and to judge it from a modern perspective, often feeling morally superior. This, indeed, is how Roman games were typically discussed up through the middle of the twentieth century, before more objective studies were undertaken. One might hear a visitor at the Colosseum today in one breath marvel at the colossal size of the building and decry the cruelty of the games in the next, saying that nothing like that could happen today, for our morals and the values placed on human life have evolved. In courses that deal with the subject of the Roman games, students sometimes vocalize similar thoughts. Nonetheless, we must recognize that there was absolutely nothing inherently "cruel," "evil," or "brutal" about Roman civilization. Their cultural and social outlook simply allowed for a certain type of institutionalized violence, and the institutionalization of violence still exists in the modern world, though enacted in different ways. We must not forget that it was our epoch, the twentieth century, which saw the greatest cruelties humans had ever inflicted upon each other: global wars, genocides, and the Holocaust. Genocides and international conflicts have continued into the twenty-first century.

The Roman amphitheater was a microcosm of Roman social order where Roman notions of power and cultural superiority were played out. Citizens watched slaves, foreigners, and condemned criminals perform and die for their amusement. Such groups were dehumanized by privileged citizens, and their lives consequently held far less value in the eyes of spectators. The nineteenth-century concept of Manifest Destiny maintained a God-given American cultural superiority, in the name of which Native American populations were displaced and exterminated. It would be difficult to argue that nineteenth-century Americans were inherently "cruel" or "evil," but the concept allowed for a certain type of institutionalized violence against a different race of people who inhabited the continent prior to colonization. Relatable to Manifest Destiny, and espoused in some circles today, is the concept of American Exceptionalism, which maintains a nationalistic sense of political and cultural superiority over all other countries in the world.

Consider how immigrants, noncitizens, and religious, ethnic, racial, and nonheteronormative minority populations are treated in contemporary culture and scapegoated for society's ills in several industrialized nations at the time of this writing. In an age of increasing tribalism, we might reflect on the vitriolic mantras and rhetoric repeated by certain political leaders now, even in modern Western democracies, and how it contributes to the dehumanization and "othering" of people, which results in less collective empathy and excuses treatment that majority populations, and the leaders that they prop up, would never tolerate for themselves. The present is never perfectly analogous to the past, but we do not have to dig deep before we start to see parallels.

The Colosseum is a magnificent structure, truly one of the largest and most elaborate monuments that the Romans ever built; as Martial says in flattering the emperor, it must have been a marvelous site to behold when it was new, on par with the Seven Wonders of the Ancient World. For the Flavian emperors, it was the crowning achievement of a politicized building program that promoted dynastic legitimacy and communicated their long-term ambitions; it was also the locus for the spectacular deaths of those whom Roman society marginalized. The Colosseum stands today as an enduring testament to Roman imperial power, engineering prowess, vision, and a civilization's ability to marshal resources; it reminds us of everything that humanity can accomplish and of which it is also capable.

ACKNOWLEDGMENTS

Thanks are owed to several people and entities, for without their help the realization of this book would have been greatly hindered. First, I am grateful to my academic dean, Lee Nordt, who kindly subsidized my travel to Rome in October 2017 so that I could reexamine aspects of the Colosseum and shoot many of the photographs that appear as illustrations in this book. Thanks to Lee, I was able to stay at a hotel conveniently located next to the Colosseum, and overlooking the Ludus Magnus, as I worked intensively on these goals over the course of a week. He, my associate dean, Kim Kellison, and my department chair, Mark Anderson, have been constant in their support and encouragement of my research and their enthusiasm for this project. My colleagues in Art History and Classics have also encouraged this project, specifically Sean DeLouche, Heidi Hornik, and Karen Pope. Karen generously proofread chapters prior to submission, and Sean commented on some of the content as I was mulling it over. Although I had worked on various aspects of the Colosseum for many years and a book on the subject was in the back of my mind, I resolved to formulate a proposal and begin work in spring 2017 after a brief conversation with Heidi. She asked what was next after my last book was completed; I responded that the Colosseum might be a natural topic for the next book. After verbalizing it, I could not banish thoughts of this book from my mind and soon thereafter formulated a proposal and sample chapter for Johns Hopkins University Press.

Allbritton Art Institute Grants for Faculty Scholarship helped to pay for image reproduction and image licensing and to produce an index. I also wish to acknowledge Elisabeth Wolfe, who has composed the index for three of my books now; in each case, she has done a superior job. I commissioned Cade Kegerreis, a talented former studio-art student, to create four drawings and plans that appear in this book. My colleague Jennings Sheffield processed and retouched many of my photographs, and Lisa Fehsenfeld, my department's gifted visual resources curator, also checked the quality of many of my images, retouched some images, and offered her expertise numerous times on a variety of technical questions. Their contributions enhanced the quality of the final product.

I am grateful to Steven L. Tuck, at Miami University, for making his research on the sculptural programs in the façades of amphitheaters available to me prior to publication. I owe thanks also to Sinclair Bell, at Northern Illinois University, who provided encouragement and excellent feedback on the manuscript, especially with regard to issues that involved the Circus Maximus.

Greg Aldrete, the Witness to Ancient History series editor, kindly read and commented on drafts of the chapters as I prepared them. He was enthusiastic about the book proposal from the very beginning and always encouraging and helpful, as was Matthew McAdam, my editor at Johns Hopkins University Press; Matt was also excited about the prospect of the first book on a monument for the series. Their expertise and judgment helped me to craft a better book. The apt feedback of the referees also improved the quality of the content. I received the final reviews while on a Margo Tytus Fellowship at the University of Cincinnati. Access to the university's superior Classics Library and the flexibility of the fellowship allowed me the time and resources to make timely revisions to the manuscript. Steven Ellis, director of the Tytus Fellowship program, and the Classics faculty, graduate students, and library personnel were generous and wonderful hosts.

Finally, I would like to acknowledge the students in my undergraduate seminar on the Colosseum in spring 2018. Over the course of fifteen weeks, we intensively studied and discussed the many dimensions of the Colosseum and its spectacles. Their indulgence in this special-topics seminar allowed me to keep the Colosseum on my mind throughout the long semester, when writing and research are difficult to accomplish because of teaching responsibilities, committee work, and unending meetings; the seminar also allowed me to think about the final organization and content of the book for an undergraduate audience. These excellent and hard-working students merit recognition by name: Joseph Brennan, Holly Draper, Sakina Haji, Edith Juanah, Joshua Kim, Joshua Martin, and Noah Martella. Each of them is now a Colosseum expert.

NOTES

PROLOGUE. **OPENING DAY AT THE COLOSSEUM**

1. Martial, *Book of Spectacles* 11 (9); 22 (19).
2. Martial, *Book of Spectacles* 9 (7).
3. Suetonius, *Deified Vespasian* 9.1.

CHAPTER 1. **THE RISE OF A NEW DYNASTY**

1. Suetonius, *Nero* 38. Cassius Dio 62.16 and Pliny, *Natural History* 17.5, also rumored that the cause of the fire was arson at Nero's command. For discussion and presentation of various sources relating to the Great Fire, see A. A. Barrett, E. Fantham, and J. C. Yardley (eds.), *The Emperor Nero: A Guide to the Ancient Sources* (Princeton: Princeton University Press, 2016) 149–170. Also see the essay by C. Panella, "Nerone e il grande incendio del 64 d.C.," in M. A. Tomei and R. Rea (eds.), *Nerone* (Milan: Electa, 2011) 76–91.
2. Tacitus, *Annals* 15.38–39. He also writes that a rumor had spread that Nero was singing while Rome burned.
3. Tacitus, *Annals* 15.43; Suetonius, *Nero* 16.1. On Nero's reforms, see also M. Griffin, *Nero: The End of a Dynasty* (New Haven: Yale University Press, 1984) 130–131.
4. Tacitus, *Annals* 12.66–67; Suetonius, *Deified Claudius* 44; Cassius Dio 61.34. For more on Agrippina, see A. A. Barrett, *Agrippina: Sex, Power, and Politics in the Early Empire* (New Haven: Yale University Press, 1996).
5. Tacitus, *Annals* 13.16.
6. Tacitus, *Annals* 14.4–8; Suetonius, *Nero* 34; Cassius Dio 62.12–14.
7. For a recent book on the Praetorian Guard and the role it could play in imperial politics and the succession, see G. de la Bédoyère, *Praetorian: The Rise and Fall of Rome's Imperial Body Guard* (New Haven: Yale University Press, 2017).
8. Suetonius, *Deified Vespasian* 4.4. Tacitus, *Annals* 16.5.3, states that Vespasian fell asleep when Nero was performing during the Second Neronia in 65 CE.
9. Suetonius, *Nero* 49.
10. The Julio-Claudian dynasty was founded by the first emperor, Augustus (grand-nephew of Julius Caesar, and his son by adoption), and joined with the Claudian family by his marriage to Livia and his adoption of her son, Tiberius, who would succeed him as emperor.
11. The events of 68 and 69 CE, after Nero's death, are complex. For fuller detail, see H. Grassl, *Untersuchungen zum Vierkaiserjahr 68/69 n. Chr. Ein Beitrag zur Ideologie und Sozialstruktur des frühen Prinzipats* (Vienna: Verband der Wissenschaftlichen Gesellschaften

Österreichs Verlag, 1973); C. L. Murison, *Galba, Otho and Vitellius: Careers and Controversies* (Hildesheim: Georg Olms, 1993); G. Morgan, *69 AD: The Year of the Four Emperors* (Oxford: Oxford University Press, 2006); M. R. Panetta, "Fine di una dinastia: la morte di Nerone," in Tomei and Rea (eds.), *Nerone*, 26–35.

12. Tacitus, *Histories* 3.71–72.

13. An excellent exploration of Vespasian's career, his reign, and his legacy is B. Levick, *Vespasian* (London: Routledge, 1999). Also important is F. Coarelli (ed.), *Divus Vespasianus: Il bimillenario dei Flavi* (Milan: Electa, 2009). For Titus, see B. W. Jones, *The Emperor Titus* (London: St. Martin's Press, 1984). For Domitian, see B. W. Jones, *Domitian and the Senatorial Order: A Prosopographical Study of Domitian's Relationship with the Senate* (Philadelphia: American Philosophical Society, 1979); B. W. Jones, *The Emperor Domitian* (London: Routledge, 1992); U. Morelli, *Domiziano: Fine di una dinastia* (Wiesbaden: Harrasowitz Verlag, 2014). For some important works on the history of the Flavian era, see C. Salles, *La Rome des Flaviens: Vespasien, Titus, Domitien* (Paris: Perrin, 2002); A. J. Boyle and W. J. Dominik (eds.), *Flavian Rome: Culture, Image, Text* (Leiden: Brill, 2003); N. Kramer and C. Reitz (eds.), *Tradition und Erneuerung. Mediale Strategien in der Zeit der Flavier* (Berlin: De Gruyter, 2010); A. Zissos (ed.), *A Companion to the Flavian Age of Imperial Rome* (Malden, MA: Wiley-Blackwell, 2016).

14. On the tax for the maintenance of the Temple in Jerusalem, see Exodus 30:13. On Vespasian's redirecting of that tax to the Temple of Jupiter Optimus Maximus, see Josephus, *Jewish War* 7.218; Cassius Dio 65.7.2.

15. Suetonius, *Deified Vespasian* 23.3; Cassius Dio 65.14.

16. L. Richardson Jr., *A New Topographical Dictionary of Ancient Rome* (Baltimore: Johns Hopkins University Press, 1992) 221–224; S. De Angeli, "Iuppiter Optimus Maximus Capitolinus, Aedes (fasi tardo-repubblicane e di età imperiale)," in M. Steinby (ed.), *Lexicon Topographicum Urbis Romae*, vol. 3, *H–O* (Rome: Edizioni Quasar, 1996) 148–153; R. Darwall-Smith, *Emperors and Architecture: A Study of Flavian Rome* (Brussels: Collection Latomus 231, 1996) 41–47.

17. An important book on the Flavian building program is Darwall-Smith, *Emperors and Architecture*. A forthcoming book by D. A. Conlin, *Political Art in Flavian Rome* (Cambridge: Cambridge University Press), will focus on the reign of Domitian.

18. For the inscriptions, see *Corpus Inscriptionum Latinarum* 6.1257–1258. On the aqueducts, see also Richardson, *A New Topographical Dictionary*, 11 and 16–17; Z. Mari, "Anio Novus" and "Aqua Claudia," in M. Steinby (ed.), *Lexicon Topographicum Urbis Romae*, vol. 1, *A–C* (Rome: Edizioni Quasar, 1993) 42–44 and 63–64.

19. For a general introduction to the Domus Aurea, see E. Segala and I. Sciortino, *Domus Aurea* (Milan: Electa, 1999). A more detailed study of the palace and its architectural features and innovation is L. F. Ball, *The Domus Aurea and the Roman Architectural Revolution* (Cambridge: Cambridge University Press, 2003). Still useful is A. Boethius, *The Golden House of Nero* (Ann Arbor: University of Michigan Press, 1960). See also A. Cassatella, "Domus Aurea," A. Cassatella and S. Panella, "Domus Aurea: vestibulum," C. Panella, "Domus Aurea: area dello stagnum," E. Papi, "Domus Aurea: porticus triplices miliariae," L. Fabbrini, "Domus Aurea: palazzo sull'Esquilino," and A. Cassatella, "Domus Aurea: complesso del Palatino," in M. Steinby (ed.), *Lexicon Topographicum Urbis Romae*, vol. 2, *D–G* (Rome: Edizioni Quasar, 1995) 49–64, for the various parts of the Domus Aurea and further references. Richardson, *A New Topographical Dictionary*, 119–121 also provides a

useful summary of the Domus Aurea, although it is supplanted by the *Lexicon Topographicum Urbis Romae* and more recent scholarship. Darwall-Smith, *Emperors and Architecture*, 35–41, surveys the Domus Aurea as prelude to the Flavian response through demolition, rebuilding, and repurposing. A recent exploration is A. La Rocca, "Staging Nero: Public Imagery and the *Domus Aurea*," in S. Bartsch, K. Freudenburg, and C. Littlewood (eds.), *The Cambridge Companion to the Age of Nero* (Cambridge: Cambridge University Press, 2017) 195–212.

20. Tacitus, *Annals* 15.42.

21. Pliny, *Natural History* 35.120.

22. Suetonius, *Nero* 39.2. The translation is from the 1950 Loeb edition (J. C. Rolfe).

23. Suetonius, *Nero* 31. The translation is from the 1950 Loeb edition (J. C. Rolfe).

24. For the Colossus of Nero, see Richardson, *A New Topographical Dictionary*, 93–94; C. Lega, "Colossus: Nero," in Steinby (ed.), *Lexicon Topographicum Urbis Romae*, vol. 1, A–C, 295–298; M. Bergmann, *Der Koloß Neros, die Domus Aurea und der Mentalitätswandel im Rom der frühen Kaiserzeit* (Mainz: Verlag Philipp von Zabern, 1993); M. Bergmann, *Die Strahlen der Herrscher* (Mainz: Verlag Philipp von Zabern, 1998), esp. 190; M. Bergmann, "Portraits of Nero, the Sun, and Roman *Otium*," in E. Buckley and M. T. Dinter (eds.), *A Companion to the Neronian Age* (Malden, MA: Wiley-Blackwell, 2013) 332–362; Darwall-Smith, *Emperors and Architecture*, 68; F. C. Albertson, "Zenodorus's 'Colossus of Nero,'" *Memoirs of the American Academy in Rome* 46 (2001) 95–118.

25. Suetonius, *Deified Vespasian* 18; Pliny, *Natural History* 34.45.

26. Griffin, *Nero*, 139.

27. Pliny, *Natural History* 36.162. This discussion of the public aspects of the Domus Aurea draws primarily from Griffin, *Nero*, 138–142.

28. Martial, *Book of Spectacles* 2. The translation is from K. M. Coleman, *Martial: Liber Spectaculorum* (Oxford: Oxford University Press, 2006) 14.

29. See K. Welch, *The Roman Amphitheatre: From Its Origins to the Colosseum* (Cambridge: Cambridge University Press, 2007) 151–153.

CHAPTER 2. A MODERN AMPHITHEATER IN ANCIENT ROME

1. The bibliography dedicated to the Colosseum is vast. Some important monographs and edited books include G. Lugli, *Roma antica. Il centro monumentale* (Rome: G. Bardi, 1946) 319–346; G. Lugli, *L'Anfiteatro Flavio* (Rome: G. Bardi, 1971); G. Cozzo, *The Colosseum: The Flavian Amphitheatre, Architecture, Building Techniques, History of the Construction, Plan of Works* (Rome: Fratelli Palombi Editori, 1971); A. M. Reggiani (ed.), *Anfiteatro Flavio. Immagine, testimonianze, spettacoli* (Rome: Edizioni Quasar, 1988); J.-C. Golvin, *L'Amphithéâtre romain. Essai sur la théorisation de sa forme et de ses fonctions*, 2 vols. (Paris: De Boccard, 1988) esp. 173–180; R. Luciani, *The Colosseum: Architecture, History and Entertainment in the Flavian Amphitheatre, Ancient Rome's Most Famous Building* (Novara: Istituto Geografico De Agostini, 1990); R. Luciani, *Il Colosseo* (Novara: Istituto Geografico De Agostini/Fenice, 1993); R. Rea, *Anfiteatro Flavio* (Rome: Istituto Polografico e Zecca dello Stato, 1996); Darwall-Smith, *Emperors and Architecture*, 76–90; D. L. Bomgardner, *The Story of the Roman Amphitheatre* (London: Routledge, 2000) 1–31; A. Gabucci (ed.), *The Colosseum*, trans. M. Becker (Los Angeles: J. Paul Getty Museum, 2000); A. La Regina (ed.), *Sangue e Arena* (Milan: Electa, 2002); R. Rea (ed.), *Rota Colisei. La valle del Colosseo attraverso I secoli* (Milan: Electa, 2002); G. Tosi, *Gli edifici per spettacoli nell'Italia romana*, 2 vols. (Rome:

Edizioni Quasar, 2003) 13–16; P. Connolly, *Colosseum: Rome's Arena of Death* (London: BBC Books, 2003); K. Hopkins and M. Beard, *The Colosseum* (Cambridge, MA: Harvard University Press, 2005); Welch, *The Roman Amphitheatre*, esp. 128–162 on the Colosseum itself; M. C. Guerrieri, *Colosseo* (Milan: Electa, 2007); N. Giustozzi, *The Colosseum Book* (Milan: Electa, 2017); R. Rea, S. Romano, and R. Santangeli Valenzani (eds.), *Colosseo* (Milan: Electa, 2017). There are also the important entries, with bibliography, in the topographical dictionaries: R. Rea, "Amphitheatrum," in Steinby (ed.), *Lexicon Topographicum Urbis Romae*, vol. 1, *A–C*, 30–35 and Richardson, *A New Topographical Dictionary*, 7–10. A useful overview of the Colosseum and its components is provided by R. Dunkle, *Gladiators: Violence and Spectacle in Ancient Rome* (Harlow: Pearson, 2008) 256–287.

2. On the reconstruction of the inscription, see G. Alföldy, "Eine Bauinschrift aus dem Colosseum," *Zeitschrift für Papyrologie und Epigraphik* 109 (1995) 195–216. For Martial's use of *amphitheatrum*, see, e.g., *Book of Spectacles* 1.7 and 2.5; for Suetonius's use of *amphitheatrum*, see, e.g., *Deified Vespasian* 9.1; *Deified Titus* 7.3.

3. The plan seems to have adorned a wall in the Temple of Peace and measured approximately 60 feet by 43 feet. As an introduction to the Forma Urbis Romae, see G. Carettoni, *La pianta marmorea di Roma antica. Forma urbis Roma* (Rome: Comune di Roma, 1960); E. Rodríguez Almeida, *Forma Urbis Marmorea: Aggiornamento Generale 1980* (Rome: Edizioni Quasar, 1981); E. Rodríguez Almeida, *Forma Urbis Antiquae. Le mappe marmoree di Roma tra la Reppublica e Settimio Severo* (Rome: École française de Rome, 2002). See also the *Stanford Digital Forma Urbis Romae Project* (http://formaurbis.stanford.edu/index.html), which contains a database and provides further bibliography. For fragments of the Colosseum, see Rodríguez Almeida, *Forma Urbis Marmorea*, fragment nos. 13 a–o.

4. For discussion of the Colosseum's name, from antiquity to the present, see Coleman, *Martial: Liber Spectaculorum*, lxvi–lxviii.

5. The claim that the Colosseum was built with Jewish slave labor derives from a statement made by G. Cozzo, *Ingeneria romana* (Rome: Libreria Editrice Mantegazza di Paolo Cremonese, 1928) 215. K. M. Coleman, "Euergetism in Its Place: Where Was the Amphitheatre in Augustan Rome?," in T. Cornell and K. Lomas (eds.), *Bread and Circuses: Euergetism and Municipal Patronage in Roman Italy* (London: Routledge) 70 and 80, n. 45, points out the source for the claim and the lack of ancient evidence for it, although she maintains it is a sensible suggestion.

6. For technical discussion of the design principles of the layout and its effect on visibility for spectators, see M. Wilson Jones, "Designing Amphitheatres," *Mitteilungen des Deutschen Archäologischen Instituts, Römische Abteilung* 100 (1993) 391–442.

7. The idea that the origin of the shape of later stone amphitheaters is found in the wooden amphitheater in Rome's Forum was first proposed by Golvin, *L'Amphithéâtre romain*, 18–21. Welch, *The Roman Amphitheatre*, 30–71 discusses wooden amphitheaters and especially the one erected in the Forum Romanum; further references are in her notes.

8. E.g., Coleman, *Martial: Liber Spectaculorum*, lxx; Welch, *The Roman Amphitheatre*, 107–108.

9. There is much literature on the building and engineering of the Colosseum. Some important examples include Cozzo, *Ingeneria romana*, 195–253; Cozzo, *The Colosseum*; Lugli, *Roma antica*, 319–346; Lugli, *L'Anfiteatro Flavio*; F. Sear, *Roman Architecture* (Ithaca, NY: Cornell University Press, 1982) 135–144, contains an accessible discussion, distills much of

the earlier Italian scholarship, and provides good illustrations; Luciani, *Il Colosseo*, 16–41; Golvin, *L'Amphithéâtre romain*, 175–176; Rea, *Anfiteatro Flavio*; Bomgardner, *The Story of the Roman Amphitheatre*, 25–31; L. Lancaster, "The Process of Building the Colosseum: The Site, Materials, and Construction Techniques," *Journal of Roman Archaeology* 18 (2005) 57–82.

10. H. Kähler, "Parerga zu einer Arbeit über den römischen Triumph- und Ehrenbogen," *Mitteilungen des Deutschen Archäologischen Instituts, Römische Abteilung* 54 (1939) 262–265; R. Rea, "Le antiche raffigurazioni," 37–40, in Reggiani (ed.), *Anfiteatro Flavio*.

11. On the inscription, see Alföldy, "Eine Bauinschrift aus dem Colosseum." It is also discussed and illustrated in Coleman, *Martial: Liber Spectaculorum*, lxv–lxvi, and in various other studies on the Colosseum. The original dedicatory inscription was discovered on fragments of a block inscribed for another purpose in the fifth century CE. Circular indentations on the surface of the stone are points where the original bronze letters were affixed that formed the dedicatory inscription of Titus. The original text reads "The Emperor Titus Caesar Vespasian Augustus Commanded the New Amphitheater to be Built from the Spoils of War," I[MP] T CAES VESPASI[ANVS AVG] | AMPHITHEATRV[M NOVVM] | [EX] MANVBIS [FIERI IVSSIT]; the T for Titus's name is crowded next to the C in CAES, suggesting it was inserted after Vespasian died to change the agency to Titus rather than Vespasian. The inscription is presently on display within the Colosseum.

12. David Hendin, *Guide to Biblical Coins*, 5th ed. (New York: Amphora, 2010) 412–413.

13. On the Colosseum section of the relief from the Tomb of the Haterii, see F. Castagnoli, "Gli edifici rappresentati in un rilievo del sepolcro degli Haterii," *Bullettino della Commissione Archeologica Comunale di Roma* 69 (1941) 59–69; Rea, "Le antiche raffigurazioni," 25; W. M. Jensen, "The Sculptures from the Tomb of the Haterii" (Ph.D. dissertation, University of Michigan, 1978) esp. 120–130, 137–138, who provides an extensive bibliography.

14. Jensen, "The Sculptures from the Tomb of the Haterii," 137–138.

15. Martial, *Book of Spectacles* 7.

16. These ideas about the sculptural decoration of the amphitheaters at Puteoli and Capua come from papers delivered by S. L. Tuck at the Annual Meeting of the Archaeological Institute of America in Chicago in 2014 and at the Annual Meeting of the Classical Association of the Middle West and South in Iowa City in 2013. He is preparing the research for publication. On the Capua reliefs, see S. L. Tuck, "Spectacle and Ideology in the Relief Decorations of the Anfiteatro Campano at Capua," *Journal of Roman Archaeology* 20 (2007) 255–272.

17. Tertullian, *Apology* 15.4–5; Lucillius, *Palatine Anthology* 11.184.

18. Cozzo, *The Colosseum*, 79–86; A. von Gerkan, "Die Obergeschoss des flavischen Amphitheaters," *Mitteilungen des Deutschen Archäologischen Instituts, Römische Abteilung* 40 (1925) 11–50; Rea, "Le antiche raffigurazioni," 30–37; Darwall-Smith, *Emperors and Architecture*, 78–79 and 215–216.

19. Images of buildings on Roman coins were not literal representations of buildings. For discussion, with further bibliography, see N. T. Elkins, *Monuments in Miniature: Architecture on Roman Coinage* (New York: American Numismatic Society, 2015) 1–2.

20. Cassius Dio 79.25.2–3. On the fire and reconstruction after 217 CE, see primarily L. Lancaster, "Reconstructing the Restorations of the Colosseum after the Fire of 217,"

Journal of Roman Archaeology 11 (1998) 146–174, and, earlier, von Gerkan, "Die Obergeschoss des flavischen Amphitheaters."

21. See Lancaster, "Reconstructing the Restorations," 162–165, figs. 23–26, for ground plans of each level that show the extent of the Severan reconstruction.

22. The awning is discussed in several of the studies cited in note 1 in this chapter. See also R. Graefe, *Vela erunt. Die Zeltdächer der römischen Theater und ähnlicher Anlagen*, 2 vols. (Mainz: von Zabern, 1979), esp. 56–96, on the Colosseum and other amphitheaters.

23. Pliny, *Natural History* 19.23; Cassius Dio 43.24.2.

24. Suetonius, *Caligula* 26.5.

25. *Corpus Inscriptionum Latinarum* 4.7993. For the translation, see A. Cooley and M. G. L. Cooley, *Pompeii and Herculaneum: A Sourcebook* (London: Routledge, 2013) 72; they also survey and translate similar advertisements.

26. Lucretius 4.75–80; Pliny, *Natural History* 19.24; Cassius Dio 63.6.2.

27. On the evidence of the Castra Misenatum in Rome and evidence for the marines who looked after the awnings in the Colosseum and other buildings, see Richardson, *A New Topographical Dictionary*, 77–78; D. Palombi, "Castra Misenatum," in Steinby (ed.), *Lexicon Topographicum Urbis Romae*, vol. 1, A–C, 248–249.

28. Much of what is discussed here regarding seating capacity and seating arrangements is not without some debate and disagreement; see the various sources in note 1 as a starting point.

29. Pliny, *Natural History* 36.102.

30. For security in Rome during and at the games, see A. Scobie, "Spectator Security and Comfort at Gladiatorial Games," *Nikephoros* 1 (1988) 191–243; S. Bingham, "Security at the Games in the Early Imperial Period," *Echos du Monde Classique* 43 (1999) 369–379.

31. E.g., Martial, *Book of Spectacles* 3; 27 (24). See also the commentary of Coleman, *Martial: Liber Spectaculorum*.

32. Seneca, *On Benefits* 7.12.24.

33. Cicero, *For Lucius Murena* 40; Velleius Paterculus 2.32.3.

34. On this point, and with reference to several ancient sources, see Dunkle, *Gladiators*, 263–264.

35. Suetonius, *Deified Augustus* 44.1. See also E. Rawson, "*Discrimina Ordinum*: The *Lex Julia Theatralis*," *Papers of the British School at Rome* 55 (1987) 83–114.

36. Bomgardner, *The Story of the Roman Amphitheatre*, 17, suggests the tiers of seats on the podium were added in late antiquity to accommodate the increased size of the Senate; he estimates that the seven tiers of seats could accommodate up to 1,750 spectators.

37. See Suetonius, *Deified Augustus* 44.2, where those wearing the *pullus* are placed at the back of the theater.

38. *Corpus Inscriptionum Latinarum* 6.32363. For some further discussion of the inscription, with additional bibliography, see Bomgardner, *The Story of the Roman Amphitheatre*, 18–20; S. Orlandi, "Seating Inscriptions for the *Fratres Arvales*," in Gabucci (ed.), *The Colosseum*, 126.

39. Suetonius, *Nero* 12.2.

40. Suetonius, *Deified Augustus* 44.3.

41. Lugli, *Roma Antica*, 330; Lugli, *L'Anfiteatro Flavio*, 23–25.

42. Cassius Dio 73.4.

43. I. Iacopi, "Il passaggio sotterraneo cosiddetto di Commodo," in La Regina (ed.), *Sangue e arena*, 79–87.

44. Coleman, *Martial: Liber Spectaculorum*, lxxii, n. 155.

45. On the identification of the emperor's box on the northern side, see N. T. Elkins, "Locating the Imperial Box in the Flavian Amphitheatre: The Numismatic Evidence," *Numismatic Chronicle* 164 (2004) 147–157; for further discussion on the identification and function of the southern platform as the *pulvinar*, see N. T. Elkins, "The Procession and Placement of Imperial Cult Images in the Colosseum," *Papers of the British School at Rome* 82 (2014) 73–107. On small sculptures carried in Roman processions, see B. Madigan, *The Ceremonial Sculptures of the Roman Gods* (Leiden: Brill, 2013).

46. Cassius Dio 76.25.3.

47. For the capacity estimate, see Bomgardner, *The Story of the Roman Amphitheatre*, 20, table 1.2.

48. B. L. Damsky, "The Throne and Curule Chair types of Titus and Domitian," *Schweizerische Numismatische Rundschau* 74 (1995) 59–73, first argued the association of these coins with the Colosseum's dedication. Elkins, "The Procession and Placement," further develops their association with the Colosseum.

49. For reconstructions of how the arena floor was laid over the substructures, see H.-J. Beste, "The Construction and Phases of Development of the Wooden Arena Flooring of the Colosseum," *Journal of Roman Archaeology* 13 (2000) 79–92.

50. There is a vast and technical bibliography on the substructures in the Colosseum. In addition to the general information in the sources cited in note 1, see particularly the work of Heinz-Jürgen Beste: e.g., "Relazione sulle indagini in corso nei sotterranei, i cosiddetti ipogei," *Mittelungen des Deutschen Archäologsichen Instituts, Römische Abteilung* 105 (1998) 106–118; "Neue Forschungsergebnisse zu einem Aufzugssystem im Untergeschoß des Kolosseums," *Mittelungen des Deutschen Archäologsichen Instituts, Römische Abteilung* 106 (1999) 249–276; "I sotterranei del Colosseo: impianto, trasformazioni e funzionamento," in La Regina (ed.), *Sangue e arena*, 277–299.

51. An excellent and accessible overview of the drains, fountains, and toilets in the Colosseum—with color-coded plans and high-quality photographs—is L. Lombardi, "The Water System," in Gabucci (ed.), *The Colosseum*, 234–240. See also Rea, *Anfiteatro Flavio*, 104–107.

52. On saffron sprays in amphitheaters and theaters, the mechanisms by which they were distributed, and their effects, see J. Day, "Scents of Place and Colours of Smell: Fragranced Entertainment in Ancient Rome," in E. Betts (ed.), *Senses of the Empire: Multisensory Approaches to Roman Culture* (London: Routledge, 2017) 176–192.

53. Martial, *Book of Spectacles* 3.8; See the commentary of Coleman, *Martial: Liber Spectaculorum*, 47–48.

54. For illustrations and discussion of such fragments and their significance, see P. Pensabene, "Elementi architettonici in marmo," 53–82, in Reggiani (ed.), *Anfiteatro Flavio*.

55. Many of the sources cited in note 1 discuss stucco and other forms of decoration and adornment in the Colosseum. For a detailed study of the stuccowork, see N. Dacos, "Les stucs du Colisée. Vestiges archéologiques et dessins de la Renaissance," *Latomus* 21.2 (1962) 334–355; E. Paparatti, "Osservazioni sugli stucchi," in Reggiani (ed.), *L'Anfiteatro Flavio*, 83–89.

CHAPTER 3. AN AMPHITHEATER IN THE HEART OF ROME

1. On this amphitheater, see Richardson, *A New Topographical Dictionary*, 11; A. Viscogliosi, "Amphitheatrum Statilii Tauri," in Steinby (ed.), *Lexicon Topographicum Urbis Romae*, vol. 1, A–C, 36–37; Welch, *The Roman Amphitheatre*, 108–127.

2. Richardson, *A New Topographical Dictionary*, 6–7 (Caligula) and 10–11 (Nero); D. Palombi, "Amphitheatrum Caligulae" and "Amphitheatrum Neronis," in Steinby (ed.), *Lexicon Topographicum Urbis Rome*, vol. 1, A–C, 35–36.

3. On the Flavian building program, see Darwall-Smith, *Emperors and Architecture*.

4. On the Temple of Claudius, see Richardson, *A New Topographical Dictionary*, 87–88; C. Buzetti, "Claudius, Divus, Templum," in Steinby (ed.), *Lexicon Topographicum Urbis Romae*, vol. 1, A–C, 277–288; Darwall-Smith, *Emperors and Architecture*, 48–55.

5. Richardson, *A New Topographical Dictionary*, 286–287; F. Coarelli, "Pax, Templum," in M. Steinby (ed.), *Lexicon Topographicum Urbis Romae*, vol. 4, P–S, 67–70; Darwall-Smith, *Emperors and Architecture*, 55–68; and, especially P. L. Tucci, *The Temple of Peace in Rome*, 2 vols. (Cambridge: Cambridge University Press, 2017).

6. Suetonius, *Deified Titus* 7.3; Cassius Dio 66.25.1. Richardson, *A New Topographical Dictionary*, 396–397; G. Caruso, "Thermae Titi/Titianae," in M. Steinby (ed.), *Lexicon Topographicum Urbis Romae*, vol. 5, T–Z (Rome: Edizioni Quasar, 1999) 66–67; Darwall-Smith, *Emperors and Architecture*, 90–94.

7. Suetonius, *Deified Titus* 8.2.

8. A. M. Colini, "Meta Sudans," *Rendiconti della Pontificia Accademia Romana di Archeologia* 13 (1937) 15–39; Richardson, *A New Topographical Dictionary*, 253; C. Panella (ed.), *Meta Sudans I. Un'area sacra in Palatio e la valle del Colosseo prima e dopo Nerone* (Rome: Istituto Poligrafico e Zecca dello Stato, 1996); C. Panella, "Meta Sudans," in Steinby (ed.), *Lexicon Topographicum Urbis Romae*, vol. 3, H–O, 247–249; B. Longfellow, "Reflections on Imperialism: The Meta Sudans in Rome and the Provinces," *Art Bulletin* 92 (2010) 275–292; B. Longfellow, *Roman Imperialism and Civic Patronage: Form, Meaning, and Ideology in Monumental Fountain Complexes* (Cambridge: Cambridge University Press, 2011) esp. 23–25, 31–48.

9. M. Pfanner, *Der Titusbogen* (Mainz: von Zabern, 1983); Richardson, *A New Topographical Dictionary*, 30; J. Arce, "Arcus Titi (Via Sacra)," in Steinby (ed.), *Lexicon Topographicum Urbis Romae*, vol. 1, A–C, 109–111; D. E. E. Kleiner, *Roman Sculpture* (New Haven: Yale University Press, 1992) 183–191. Another arch of Titus was incorporated into the Circus Maximus, the remains of which have been recently excavated and published; see M. Buonfiglio, S. Pergola, and G. L. Zanzi, "The Hemicycle of the Circus Maximus: Synthesis of the Late Antique Phases Revealed by Recent Investigations," *Memoirs of the American Academy in Rome* 61 (2016) 279–303.

10. As an introduction to the triumph, see M. Beard, *The Roman Triumph* (Cambridge, MA: Harvard University Press, 2007).

11. For these gladiator schools, see Richardson, *A New Topographical Dictionary*, 236–238; C. Pavolini, "Ludus Dacicus," "Ludus Gallicus," "Ludus Magnus," and "Ludus Matutinus," in Steinby (ed.), *Lexicon Topographicum Urbis Rome*, vol. 3, H–O, 195–198; Darwall-Smith, *Emperors and Architecture*, 218–220. For more on the Ludus Magnus specifically, see L. Cozza (ed.), *Ludus Magnus* (Rome: A. Staderini, 1962); Golvin, *L'Amphithéatre romain*, 149–152.

12. Inscriptions record that Domitian's schools were operated by equestrians in the imperial service; see *Corpus Inscriptionum Latinarum* 6.1645; 6.1647; 8.8328; 14.2922.

13. Richardson, *A New Topographical Dictionary*, 39, 342, 366, and 374; E. Rodríguez Almeida, "Armamentaria," in Steinby (ed.), *Lexicon Topographicum Urbis Romae*, vol. 1, A–C, 126; D. Palombi, "Spoliarium," C. Pavolini, "Saniarium," and K. Welch, "Summum Choragium," in Steinby (ed.), *Lexicon Topographicum Urbis Rome*, vol. 4, P–S, 338–339, 233, and 386–387. The Saniarium is called the "Samiarium" in the *Regionaries*, which has led to the suggestion that it was a place for the maintenance and sharpening of weapons. Some scholars believe what was intended was "Saniarium," which would be a hospital for gladiators, and the more sensible identification for a structure worthy of mention in the *Regionaries*.

14. Richardson, *A New Topographical Dictionary*, 77–78; D. Palombi, "Castra Misenatum."

15. For some discussion of the Flavian need to project legitimacy, and for ideological associations with Augustus and Claudius, see B. Levick, *Vespasian*, esp. 66, 71–78; A. J. Boyle, "Introduction: Reading Flavian Rome," and R. Mellor, "The New Aristocracy of Power," in Boyle and Dominik (eds.), *Flavian Rome*, 4–13 and 80–84; Jones, *The Emperor Titus*, esp. 121–122; E. Lyasse, *Le Principat et son fondateur. L'utilisation de la reference à Auguste de Tibère à Trajan* (Brussels: Collection Latomus 311, 2008) 301–328.

16. Claudius is not referred to as "Deified" in the inscription recording the decree, although Vespasian would later promote his cult. As an introduction, see P. A. Brunt, "Lex de Imperio Vespasiani," *Journal of Roman Studies* 67 (1977) 95–116; A. Pabst, ". . . *ageret faceret quaecumque e re publica censeret esse*. Annäherungen an die *Lex de Imperio Vespasiani*," in W. Dalheim (ed.), *Festschrift Robert Werner zu seinem 65. Geburtstag* (Konstanz: Universitätsverlag, 1989) 125–148; L. Dészpa, "The Flavians and the Senate," in Zissos (ed.), *A Companion to the Flavian Age*, 166–185. The *Companion*'s appendix 4, pp. 570–572, conveniently contains both the Latin text and an English translation of the inscription.

17. Suetonius, *Deified Vespasian* 7.2. The translation is from the 1950 Loeb edition (J. C. Rolfe).

18. Suetonius, *Deified Titus* 2.

19. Suetonius, *Deified Titus* 7.1.

20. For the Colosseum coins and their variants, see, primarily, N. T. Elkins, "The Flavian Colosseum *Sestertii*: Currency or Largess?," *Numismatic Chronicle* 166 (2006) 211–221.

21. Levick, *Vespasian*, 71–78.

22. On representations of the altar on coins and their ideological significance, see S. E. Cox, "The Mark of the Successor: Tribunician Power and the Ara Providentia under Tiberius and Vespasian," *Numismatica e Antichità Classiche* 34 (2005) 251–270.

23. Suetonius, *Deified Vespasian* 19.1; Cassius Dio 65.10.1.

24. Tucci, *The Temple of Peace*, 76–115.

25. See, e.g., W. J. Tatum, "Another Look at Suetonius' *Titus*," in T. Power and R. K. Gibson, *Suetonius the Biographer: Studies in Roman Lives* (Oxford: Oxford University Press, 2014) 159–177.

26. Cassius Dio 53.1.5 on Augustus's *stadium*. On the Stadium of Domitian, see A. M. Colini, *Stadium Domitiani* (Rome: Edizioni Quasar, 1998 [reprint of the 1943 edition]); Richardson, *A New Topographical Dictionary*, 366–367; P. Virgili, "Stadium Domitiani," in Steinby (ed.), *Lexicon Topographicum Urbis Romae*, vol. 4, P–S, 341–343.

27. On connections between the Circus Maximus and Stadium of Domitian, see S. Pergola and M. Buonfiglio, "Stadio di Domiziano e Circo Massimo: riflessioni sullo

svolgimento degli agoni ginnici e dei ludi circensi in relazione agli schemi progettuali dei due edifici di," *Histria Antiqua* 21 (2012) 187-198.

28. Suetonius, *Domitian* 4.2; Cassius Dio 67.8.

29. See, e.g., P. Heslin, "Augustus, Domitian and the So-Called Horologium Augusti," *Journal of Roman Studies* 97 (2007) 1-20. On parallels between Augustus and Domitian in Martial, see also L. Roman, "Martial and the City of Rome," *Journal of Roman Studies* 100 (2010) 88-117.

30. Welch, *The Roman Amphitheatre*, 130-147 and 161-162.

31. On the Theater of Marcellus, see Richardson, *A New Topographical Dictionary*, 382-383; P. Ciancio Rossetto, "Theatrum Marcelli," in Steinby (ed.), *Lexicon Topographicum Urbis Romae*, vol. 5, *T–Z*, 31-35; F. Sear, *Roman Theatres: An Architectural Study* (Oxford: Oxford University Press, 2006) 61-65 and 135-136; Tosi, *Gli edifici per spettacoli*, 25-27.

32. Golvin, *L'Amphithéâtre romain*, 179, and Sear, *Roman Theatres*, 32 draw parallels between the façades of both buildings.

33. Suetonius, *Deified Vespasian* 9.1.

34. A. Futrell, *Blood in the Arena: The Spectacle of Roman Power* (Austin: University of Texas Press, 1997) 79-93.

35. Coleman, "Euergetism in Its Place," 74-77, has helpfully collated a list of arena spectacles held during Augustus's reign.

36. P. Sabbatini Tumolesi, *Gladiatorum Paria. Annunci di spettacoli gladiatorii a Pompei* (Rome: Edizioni di Storia e Letteratura, 1980) 129-133. Also relevant to cultic activity in amphitheaters, see M. Le Glay, "Les amphithéâtres: *loci religiosi?*," in C. Domergue, C. Landes, and J.-M. Pailler (eds.), *Spectacula - I. Gladiateurs et amphithéâtres: actes du colloque tenu à Toulouse et à Lattes les 26, 27, 28 et 29 Mai 1987* (Lattes: Editions Imago Musée Archéologique Henri Prades, 1990) 217-229.

37. Tertullian, *On Spectacles* 13.

38. Elkins, "The Procession and Placement."

39. Cassius Dio 73.17.4. The translation is from the 1927 Loeb edition (E. Cary).

40. For the probability that the inaugural games celebrated the consecration of Vespasian as a god, see Damsky, "The Throne and Curule Chair Types," 68-69; H. Komnick, *Die Restitutionsmünzen der frühen Kaiserzeit* (Berlin: De Gruyter, 2001) esp. 69-72, 165-179; Elkins, "The Flavian Colosseum *Sestertii*," 215 and n. 22; Elkins, "The Procession and Placement," 104-105. On the dating of Vespasian's consecration, see K. Scott, *The Imperial Cult under the Flavians* (Stuttgart: W. Kohlhammer, 1936) 40-45; T. V. Buttrey, "Vespasian's *Consecratio* and the Numismatic Evidence," *Historia* 25 (1976) 449-457.

41. Cassius Dio 73.21.3.

CHAPTER 4. A HUNDRED DAYS OF GAMES

1. Suetonius, *Deified Titus* 7.3; Cassius Dio 66.25.

2. On amphitheater processions, see, e.g., Dunkle, *Gladiators*, 76-89; Elkins, "The Procession and Placement"; J. A. Latham, *Performance, Memory, and Processions in Ancient Rome: The Pompa Circensis from the Late Republic to Late Antiquity* (Cambridge: Cambridge University Press, 2016) 161-180.

3. Martial, *Book of Spectacles* 4 (4.1-4); 5 (4.5-6).

4. Cassius Dio 73.17.4.

5. Suetonius, *Deified Augustus* 43.5.

6. Suetonius, *Deified Titus* 9.1–2; Cassius Dio 68.3.2.

7. On *venationes* in general and in the Colosseum, see A. M. Reggiani, "La *venatio*: origine e prime raffigurazioni," in Reggiani (ed.), *Anfiteatro Flavio*, 147–155; M. Junklemann, "*Familia Gladiatoria*: The Heroes of the Amphitheatre," in E. Köhne and C. Ewigleben (eds.), *Gladiators and Caesars* (Berkeley: University of California Press, 2000) 70–74; F. Meijer, *The Gladiators: History's Most Deadly Sport* (London: Souvenir Press, 2004) 121–134, 138–147; Dunkle, *Gladiators*, esp. 78–89; Welch, *The Roman Amphitheatre*, esp. 22–29; C. Epplett, "Roman Beast Hunts," in P. Christesen and D. G. Kyle (eds.), *A Companion to Sport and Spectacle in Greek and Roman Antiquity* (Malden, MA: Wiley Blackwell, 2014) 505–519.

8. Seneca, *On the Shortness of Life* 13.3; Eutropius 2.14.5.

9. Livy 44.18.8.

10. Welch, *The Roman Amphitheatre*, esp. 22–29.

11. Valerius Maximus 2.7.13–14.

12. E.g., G. G. Fagan, *The Lure of the Arena: Social Psychology and the Crowd at the Roman Games* (Cambridge: Cambridge University Press, 2011) 246–252.

13. Dunkle, *Gladiators*, 78–82.

14. Strabo 17.1.44.

15. Pliny, *Natural History* 8.20.

16. E.g., Junkelmann, "*Familia Gladiatoria*," 71.

17. Martial, *Book of Spectacles* 8 (6b); Cassius Dio 66.25.1–2. For each citation of Martial, refer to the commentary in Coleman, *Martial: Liber Spectaculorum*.

18. On the question of whose games the *Book of Spectacles* records, and as an introduction to the debate, see Coleman, *Martial: Liber Spectaculorum*, xlv–lxiv; T. V. Buttrey, "Domitian, the Rhinoceros, and the Date of Martial's *Liber De Spectaculis*," *Journal of Roman Studies* 97 (2007) 101–112.

19. Martial, *Book of Spectacles* 14 (12)–16 (14).

20. Martial, *Book of Spectacles* 17 (15); 32 (27; 28).

21. Cassius Dio 66.25.1.

22. Martial, *Book of Spectacles* 11 (9); 26 (22 + 23). The translations are from Coleman, *Martial: Liber Spectaculorum*, 101 and 186.

23. Martial, *Book of Spectacles* 20 (17); 21 (18).

24. Martial, *Book of Spectacles* 12 (10).

25. Martial, *Book of Spectacles* 13 (11); Coleman, *Martial: Liber Spectaculorum*, 120–121.

26. Martial, *Book of Spectacles* 18 (16); 19 (16b).

27. See, e.g., R. Rea, "Gli animali per la venatio: cattura, transporto, custodia," in La Regina (ed.), *Sangue e Arena*, 245–275. M. MacKinnon, "Supplying Exotic Animals for the Roman Amphitheatre Games: New Reconstructions Combining Archaeological, Ancient Textual, Historical and Ethnographic Data," *Mouseion*, ser. 3, 6 (2006) 137–161.

28. Cassius Dio 66.25.1.

29. Tertullian, *On the Spectacles* 19; *Apology* 9.11.

30. D. G. Kyle, *Spectacles of Death in Ancient Rome* (London: Routledge, 1998) 184–212; MacKinnon, "Supplying Exotic Animals," 154–156.

31. Results of the excavations have not yet been scientifically published. Until then, see M. Gannon, "Ancient Concession Stands and Shops Found at Roman Gladiator Arena," *Live Science* (April 4, 2017), https://www.livescience.com/58521-ancient-shops-found-at-roman -gladiator-arena.html.

32. *Corpus Inscriptionum Latinarium* 4.9983a.

33. The authoritative work on Roman executions in the amphitheater is K. M. Coleman, "Fatal Charades: Roman Executions Staged as Mythological Enactments," *Journal of Roman Studies* 80 (1990) 44–73. For recent summaries of additional work, see Dunkle, *Gladiators,* 90–94; C. Epplett, "Spectacular Executions in the Roman World," in Christesen and Kyle (eds.), *A Companion to Sport and Spectacle,* 520–532.

34. Tertullian, *Apology* 15.4–5.

35. Martial, *Epigrams* 8.30; 10.25.

36. See Martial, *Book of Spectacles* 6 (5). For each execution, refer to the appropriate commentary in Coleman, "Fatal Charades" and *Martial: Liber Spectaculorum.*

37. Martial, *Book of Spectacles* 9 (7). The translation is from Coleman, *Martial: Liber Spectaculorum,* 82.

38. Martial, *Epigrams* 8.30.9–10. The translation is from the 1993 Loeb edition (D. R. Schackleton Bailey).

39. Martial, *Book of Spectacles* 10 (8). Coleman, *Martial: Liber Spectaculorum,* 97–100.

40. J. R. Clarke, *Looking at Laughter: Humor, Power, and Transgression in Roman Visual Culture, 100 BC–AD 250* (Berkeley: University of California Press, 2007) 23–25.

41. Martial, *Book of Spectacles* 24 (21).

42. The bibliography on gladiators, their combats, training, and lives is particularly vast. In general, see G. Ville, *La gladiature en occident des orgines à la mort de Domitien* (Paris: École de française de Rome, 1981); T. Wiedemann, *Emperors and Gladiators* (London: Routledge, 1992); P. Plass, *The Game of Death in Ancient Rome: Arena Sport and Political Suicide* (Madison: University of Wisconsin Press, 1995); Futrell, *Blood in the Arena*; Kyle, *Spectacles of Death*; Köhne and Ewigleben (eds.), *Gladiators and Caesars*; Meijer, *The Gladiators*; Welch, *The Roman Amphitheatre,* 11–22; Dunkle, *Gladiators*; G. G. Fagan, "Gladiatorial Combat as Alluring Spectacle," in Christesen and Kyle (eds.), *A Companion to Sport and Spectacle,* 465–477.

43. Livy, *Periochae* 16.

44. On gladiator graffiti at Pompeii, see, as an introduction, Cooley and Cooley, *Pompeii and Herculaneum,* 74–89. On the Colosseum, see P. Sabbatini Tumolesi, "Gli spettacoli anfiteatrali all luce di alcune testimonianze epigrafiche," in Reggiani (ed.), *Anfiteatro Flavio,* 91–99.

45. *Inscriptiones Latinae Selectae* 5107.

46. For an overview of different gladiator types, with some illustrations and further bibliography, see F. Coarelli, "L'armamento e le classi dei gladiatori," in La Regina (ed.), *Sangue e Arena,* 153–173; Dunkle, *Gladiators,* 98–118. Dunkle also discusses several lesser-known types that are not covered here.

47. Yale University Art Gallery, 2009.193.3, https://artgallery.yale.edu/collections/objects /79336.

48. Suetonius, *Deified Claudius* 21.6.

49. Ville, *La gladiature,* 326; Coleman, *Martial: Liber Spectaculorum,* 232–233; Dunkle, *Gladiators,* 71.

50. F. Kanz and K. Großschmidt, "Dying in the Arena: The Osseous Evidence from Ephesian Gladiators," in T. Wilmott (ed.), *Roman Amphitheatres and Spectacula: A 21st-Century Perspective* (Oxford: Archaeopress, BAR International Series 1946, 2009) 211–220.

51. Martial, *Book of Spectacles*, 7 (6); The translation is from Coleman, *Martial: Liber Spectaculorum*, 69.

52. For evidence of female gladiators in the Roman world, see Ville, *La gladiature*, 263–264; Dunkle, *Gladiators*, esp. 118–123; S. Brunet, "Women with Swords: Female Gladiators in the Roman World," in Christesen and Kyle (eds.), *A Companion to Sport and Spectacle,* 478–491.

53. Statius, *Silvae* 1.51–56. Cf. Suetonius, *Domitian* 4.1.

54. Martial, *Book of Spectacles* 31 (29; 27). The translation is from Coleman, *Martial: Liber Spectaculorum*, 218.

55. Suetonius, *Deified Titus* 8.2. The translation is from the 1950 Loeb edition (J. C. Rolfe).

56. On the flooding of the Colosseum, see primarily K. M. Coleman, "Launching into History: Aquatic Displays in the Early Empire," *Journal of Roman Studies* 83 (1993) 48–74; G. Cariou, *La Naumachie: Morituri te salutant* (Paris: Presses de l'Université Paris-Sorbonne, 2009) esp. 305–354. Cariou's book is also an excellent source on other mock naval battles and their venues. As an example of nonacceptance of the Colosseum's flooding, see Rea, "Le antiche raffigurazioni," 36–37.

57. Cassius Dio 66.25.2–4. The translation is from the 1925 Loeb edition (E. Cary).

58. Suetonius, *Domitian* 4.1. The translation is from the 1950 Loeb edition (J. C. Rolfe).

59. Martial, *Book of Spectacles* 27 (24). The translation is from Coleman, *Martial: Liber Spectaculorum*, 195.

60. Martial, *Book of Spectacles* 34 (28; 30). The translation is from Coleman, *Martial: Liber Spectaculorum*, 249.

61. Coleman, "Launching into History," 58–60.

62. Tacitus, *Annals* 4.62–63.

63. Suetonius, *Tiberius* 75.3.

64. Much recent scholarship on Roman games has begun to consider the social psychology of the crowd in viewing violent spectacles. See, most notably, Fagan, *The Lure of the Arena.*

65. Martial, *Book of Spectacles* 33 (30; 29).

66. Martial, *Book of Spectacles* 20 (17). The translation is from Coleman, *Martial: Liber Spectaculorum*, 156.

67. Cassius Dio 66.25.5. Cf. Suetonius, *Caligula* 18.1–2, who says that Caligula gave baskets of food to spectators and threw gifts to the crowd at arena games.

68. Suetonius, *Deified Titus* 8.2. The translation is from the 1950 Loeb edition (J. C. Rolfe).

CHAPTER 5. THE COLOSSEUM AND ITS FIRST GAMES
IN FLAVIAN ART AND LITERATURE

1. The most current and principal commentary on the *Book of Spectacles* is Coleman, *Martial: Liber Spectaculorum*. See her discussion throughout, but especially on pp. lxxix–lxxxi, that this work is a form of panegyric.

2. Martial, *Epigrams* 1.6.

3. Suetonius, *Domitian* 13.2; Cassius Dio 67.4.7.

4. Jones, *The Emperor Domitian*, 108–109.

5. Coleman, *Martial: Liber Spectaculorum*, liii and 159–160.

6. E.g., F. S. Kleiner, "The Trophy on the Bridge and the Roman Triumph over Nature," *L'Antiquité Classique* 60 (1991) 182–192.

7. Martial, *Book of Spectacles* 1. The translation is from Coleman, *Martial: Liber Spectaculorum*, 1.

8. Martial, *Book of Spectacles* 3. The translation is from Coleman, *Martial: Liber Spectaculorum*, 37.

9. See Coleman, *Martial: Liber Spectaculorum*, 38 and 41–42. Throughout her commentary, one finds further connections with Augustan literature. Roman, "Martial and the City of Rome," also comments on parallels between Martial's work, including the *Book of Spectacles*, and Augustan poetry and modes of praise.

10. That coin iconography served a panegyrical function was first proposed by B. Levick, "Propaganda and the Imperial Coinage," *Antichthon* 16 (1982) 104–116. Other scholars followed; e.g., see A. Wallace-Hadrill, "Image and Authority in the Coinage of Augustus," *Journal of Roman Studies* 76 (1986) 66–87. Most recently, an interdisciplinary study of Nerva's coinage has argued that coin imagery functioned as visual panegyric; see N. T. Elkins, *The Image of Political Power in the Reign of Nerva, AD 96–98* (Oxford: Oxford University Press, 2017).

11. E.g., M. Torelli, "'Ex his castra, ex his tribus replebuntur': The Marble Panegyric on the Arch of Trajan at Beneventum," in D. Buitron-Oliver (ed.), *The Interpretation of Architectural Sculpture in Greece and Rome* (Washington, DC: National Gallery of Art, 1997) 145–177; P. Stewart, *The Social History of Roman Art* (Cambridge: Cambridge University Press, 2008) 108–116; P. Zanker, *Roman Art* (Los Angles: J. Paul Getty Museum, 2010) 108–115; E. Mayer, "Propaganda, Staged Applause, or Local Politics? Public Monuments from Augustus to Septimius Severus," in B. C. Ewald and C. F. Noreña (eds.), *The Emperor and Rome: Space, Representation, and Ritual* (Cambridge: Cambridge University Press, 2010) 111–134.

12. For representations of the Colosseum on Flavian coins, see Rea, "Le antiche raffigurazioni"; Elkins, "The Flavian Colosseum *Sestertii*"; Elkins, *Monuments in Miniature*, 80–83.

13. K. M. Coleman, "Entertaining Rome," in J. N. C. Coulston and H. Dodge (eds.), *Ancient Rome: The Archaeology of the Eternal City* (Oxford: Oxford University School of Archaeology Monograph 54, 2000), 214–215.

14. Refer to the detailed commentary in Coleman, *Martial: Liber Spectaculorum*, 14–36.

15. Silius Italicus, *Punica* 3.594–596. The translation is from the 1983 Loeb edition (J. D. Duff).

16. Tatum, "Another Look at Suetonius' *Titus*."

17. Coleman, *Martial: Liber Spectaculorum*, 156–157.

18. Cassius Dio 77.1.4–5.

19. On the relationship of these texts with the image on this coin, see C. W. A. Carlson, "The 'Laetitia Temporum' Reverses of the Severan Dynasty," *Journal for the Society of Ancient Numismatics* 3 (1969) 9–11; C. Rowan, *Under Divine Auspices: Divine Ideology and the Visualisation of Imperial Power in the Severan Period* (Cambridge: Cambridge University Press, 2011) 51–52; Elkins, *The Image of Political Power*, 144–146.

20. On these, see Rea, "Le antiche raffigurazioni"; Elkins, *Monuments in Miniature*, 103–104.

21. *Augustan History, Maximinus and Balbinus* 1.3–4.

22. On the temple, see Richardson, *A New Topographical Dictionary*, 412; S. De Angeli, "Vespasianus, Divus, Templum," in Steinby (ed.), *Lexicon Topographicum Urbis Romae*, vol. 5, T–Z, 124–125.

23. On the association of this imagery with the *Book of Spectacles*, see E. Rodríguez Almeida, "Marziale in marmo," *Mélanges de l'École française de Rome: Antiquité* 106 (1994) 197–217; Coleman, *Martial: Liber Spectaculorum*, esp. 105–106.

24. *Corpus Inscriptionum Latinarum* 6.938.

EPILOGUE. THE END OF THE "FLAVIAN" AMPHITHEATER

1. Suetonius, *Deified Titus* 10.1; Cassius Dio 66.26.1.

2. On the end of gladiator combats and *venationes*, see, for example, Bomgardner, *The Story of the Roman Amphitheatre*, 197–227; G. L. Gregori, "The End of the Gladiators," in Gabucci (ed.), *The Colosseum*, 96–97; N. Christie, "No More Fun? The Ends of Entertainment Structures in the Late Roman West," in Wilmott (ed.), *Roman Amphitheatres*, 221–232; Dunkle, *Gladiators*.

3. On the notion of the Colosseum as a monument to Christian martyrs, and other aspects of its afterlife, see Rea, *Anfiteatro Flavio*, 28–67; Luciani, *Il Colosseo*, 175–241; Connolly, *Colosseum*, 153–169; Hopkins and Beard, *The Colosseum*, 149–181; Rea, Romano, and Santangeli Valenzani (eds.), *Colosseo*; Giustozzi, *The Colosseum Book*, 76–115. On the fallacy of the popular idea that there was widespread and sustained persecution of Christians by Roman authorities, see, e.g., C. Moss, *The Myth of Persecution: How Early Christians Invented a Story of Martyrdom* (New York: HarperOne, 2013).

4. Pliny, *Letters* 10.96–97.

5. On this subject, see B. D. Shaw, "The Myth of the Neronian Persecution," *Journal of Roman Studies* 105 (2015) 73–100. Tacitus, *Annals* 15.44.2 for Nero blaming the Christians.

SUGGESTED FURTHER READING

There is a vast bibliography on the Colosseum, amphitheaters, spectacles, and political history from the fall of Nero through the reigns of Vespasian, Titus, and Domitian. A great deal of essential scholarly literature is published in foreign-language sources, much of which is cited in the notes in this book. In this section, I recommend selected English-language works as further reading for the public, undergraduate students, teachers, or scholars who would like to probe more deeply the subjects explored in this book.

The Colosseum must be understood in its historical and political contexts in the aftermath of Nero's fall and the repurposing and demolition of Nero's Domus Aurea. For two key works on the reign of Nero, see Miriam T. Griffin, *Nero: The End of a Dynasty* (New Haven: Yale University Press, 1984), and Jaś Elsner and Jamie Masters (eds.), *Reflections of Nero: Culture, History, and Representation* (Chapel Hill: University of North Carolina Press, 1994). Griffin's book includes an important section on the circumstances that led to Nero's fall, and there are also important points about his building program, reforms, and the Domus Aurea. The collection of essays edited by Elsner and Masters underscores the fact that the "cruel" Nero popularly known today is largely an invention of writers and politicians of the Flavian and post-Flavian world. Elsner's chapter on "Constructing Decadence: The Representation of Nero as Imperial Builder" (112–127) is a masterful reassessment of Nero's building program and reframes it in the context of other imperial building programs; also important is his discussion of the construction of the Domus Aurea, its function, and its place in the tradition of other emperors who built palaces. Another accessible biography of Nero is David Shotter, *Nero Caesar Augustus: Emperor of Rome* (Harlow, UK: Pearson, 2008); it contains particularly useful chapters on Nero's building program and his fall from power.

In recent years, presses have published numerous handbooks and companion volumes on various periods of Roman history, primarily aimed at undergraduate and postgraduate audiences. Two recent companions will assist students in exploring the age of Nero further: Emma Buckley and Martin T. Dinter (eds.), *A Companion to the Neronian Age* (Malden, MA: Wiley-Blackwell, 2013), and Shadi Bartsch, Kirk Freudenburg, and Cedric Littlewood (eds.), *The Cambridge Companion to the Age of Nero* (Cambridge: Cambridge University Press, 2017). On the Domus Aurea more specifically, Elisabetta Segala and Ida Sciortino, *Domus Aurea* (Milan: Electa, 1999), and Axel Boethius, *The Golden House of Nero* (Ann Arbor: University of Michigan Press, 1960), provide an accessible overview of the palace and its historical context. A more detailed study of the building complex is Larry F. Ball, *The Domus Aurea and the Roman Architectural Revolution* (Cambridge: Cambridge University Press, 2003), which focuses on the physical aspects of the structure and its engineering, as well as its place in architectural history.

Engagement with primary sources is essential for those delving deeply into ancient history, but primary sources usually cannot be taken at face value and should always be read for historical inquiry in conjunction with secondary scholarly works and commentaries. For the reign of Nero, important sources are Tacitus, *Annals* 13–16; Suetonius, *Nero*; and Cassius Dio's *Roman History* 61–63. A useful new guide to these and other sources for Nero is Anthony A. Barrett, Elaine Fantham, and John C. Yardley (eds.), *The Emperor Nero: A Guide to the Ancient Sources* (Princeton: Princeton University Press, 2016). Chapters and contributions to the various books on Nero are also useful to evaluate the reliability of literary sources for Nero, and they provide citations to specialist commentaries on the primary sources and other secondary literature.

For the "Year of the Four Emperors," Gwyn Morgan, *69 AD: The Year of the Four Emperors* (Oxford: Oxford University Press, 2006), provides a thorough and engaging discussion of Nero's fall, the brief reigns of Galba, Otho, and Vitellius, and the rise of Vespasian, while Charles L. Murison, *Galba, Otho and Vitellius: Careers and Controversies* (Hildesheim: Georg Olms, 1993), covers similar ground, more focused on the three contenders. Tacitus's *Histories* is the most significant primary source for this period; also important are Suetonius's biographies: *Galba*, *Otho*, and *Vitellius*. Murison has also produced a commentary on these biographies: *Suetonius: Galba, Otho, and Vitellius* (London: Bristol Classical Press, 1993). Cassius Dio's *Roman History* 63–64 also covers 69 CE.

The amount of literature available on the Flavian emperors is immense. For a scholarly biography of Vespasian, see the masterful work by Barbara Levick, *Vespasian* (London: Routledge, 1999). Brian W. Jones, *The Emperor Titus* (London: St. Martin's Press, 1984), is the standard book on that emperor; his *The*

Emperor Domitian (London: Routledge, 1992) is also an essential reference on Domitian. There are several edited volumes dealing more broadly with various aspects of the Flavian era. Students will appreciate the accessibility and detailed bibliography, with up-to-date research, in the contributions authored by important scholars of Flavian Rome in Andrew Zissos (ed.), *A Companion to the Flavian Age of Imperial Rome* (Malden, MA: Wiley-Blackwell, 2016). Historical essays of note in that volume are "Sources and Evidence," by Frédéric Hurlet (17–39); "The Remarkable Rise of the Flavians," by Frederik Juliaan Vervaet (43–59); "The Emperor Vespasian," by John Nichols (60–75); "The Emperor Titus," by Charles L. Murison (76–91); and "The Emperor Domitian," by Alessandro Galimberti (92–108). Other important essays in the *Companion* regarding Flavian public art and building are Steven L. Tuck's "Imperial Image-Making" (109–128), Susan Wood's "Public Images of the Flavian Dynasty: Sculpture and Coinage" (129–147), and Andrew B. Gallia's "Remaking Rome" (148–165). Helen Lovatt provides an overview of "Flavian Spectacle: Paradox and Wonder" (361–375).

An exceptional contribution to the study of the Flavian period is Anthony J. Boyle and William J. Dominik (eds.), *Flavian Rome: Culture, Image, Text* (Leiden: Brill, 2003). The essays contained therein are more scholarly and advanced than the handbooks, as this book is aimed at an advanced specialist audience. It will be, nonetheless, essential to students and those who wish to pursue specific aspects of the Flavian world in greater depth. Contributions related to Flavian games include Alex Hardie, "Poetry and Politics at the Games of Domitian" (125–148), and Erik Gunderson, "The Flavian Amphitheatre: All the World as Stage" (637–658). Many contributions rely heavily on, and critically evaluate, literary sources; these will be useful for grappling with some of the problems posed by those sources. Various ancient sources are presented and commented on in M. G. L. Cooley (ed.), *The Flavians*, LACTOR 20 (London: London Association of Classical Teachers, 2015). Some important primary sources are Tacitus's *Histories*; his *Agricola*, which is critical of Domitian; Suetonius's *Deified Vespasian*, *Deified Titus*, and *Domitian*; Cassius Dio's *Roman History* 65–67; and Josephus's *Jewish War*.

An exhaustive reading list on the Colosseum itself would be a monument to produce. For advanced work, much of the literature is in foreign languages, especially Italian, and citations to many of those works can be found in the notes of this book. This book has focused squarely on the significance of the Colosseum and its spectacles during the rule of the Flavian emperors; all other books take a broader chronological approach, usually ending in the period of Late

Antiquity, the Middle Ages, or even in the nineteenth and twentieth centuries. For some of the important English-language texts on the Colosseum, I recommend beginning with Ada Gabucci (ed.), *The Colosseum* (Los Angeles: J. Paul Getty Museum, 2000). The text is translated from an Italian version, and the translation contains many typographical errors and awkward sentences, but the content was written by some of the finest Italian scholars who work on the Colosseum; among these are Rossella Rea, who was director of the Colosseum from 1985 to 2017. Anyone doing research with Italian sources will inevitably encounter her work. The book explores material and visual evidence for gladiators and arena games, and the various physical components and features of the Colosseum itself. It is lavishly illustrated in color throughout. Another richly illustrated book, with color images, is Peter Connolly's *Colosseum: Rome's Arena of Death* (London: BBC Books, 2003). Connolly surveys the ideology of the amphitheater in the Flavian age before proceeding to discussions of gladiators, their lives, *naumachiae*, and the afterlife of the Colosseum.

A good historical survey of the Colosseum is Keith Hopkins and Mary Beard, *The Colosseum* (Cambridge, MA: Harvard University Press, 2005). It is a smaller and more affordable book, but also with fewer illustrations. It, like the previous two books, is aimed at a general audience, written in an accessible way, and surveys the history of the monument from antiquity to the present. A very recent book is Nunzio Giustozzi, *The Colosseum Book* (Milan: Electa, 2017), which is presently available at the gift shop in the Colosseum. It, too, is aimed at a general audience and has a plethora of color images. Do not be deceived, however, by the title, for one will not find much on the Colosseum itself and its use in antiquity. Instead, the chapters explore, among other things, historical models of the Colosseum, gladiators, the Christian view of the Colosseum in the medieval to modern periods, the Colosseum and the Grand Tour, and the Colosseum in film. For such subjects, it is a sound introduction. There are several older guidebooks that may be difficult to find on the secondhand market and that may only be easily accessed in university libraries. A good one is Giuseppe Cozzo's *The Colosseum: The Flavian Amphitheatre* (Rome: Fratelli Palombi Editori, 1971), which is small, is well-illustrated, and has a concise and informative text on the building and its features.

Some more detailed works that treat the Colosseum do so in tandem with other amphitheaters. One of the first to recommend is David L. Bomgardner, *The Story of the Roman Amphitheatre* (London: Routledge, 2000). A whole chapter is dedicated to the Colosseum and its features, while other chapters explore the origins of the amphitheater as a building type, amphitheaters during the imperial period, North African amphitheaters, and the end of amphitheaters and their games in the later Roman Empire. It thus puts the Colosseum in a much broader architectural and historical context. Another important and recent book on amphitheaters is Katherine E. Welch, *The Roman Amphitheatre: From Its Origins to the Colosseum* (Cambridge: Cambridge University Press, 2007). The purpose of the book is to argue that the origin of Roman amphitheaters as a building type is to be found in a military context. She thus explores the military associations of animal spectacles, executions, and gladiatorial combats in the period of the Roman Republic and argues that the construction of early amphitheaters was associated with a Roman military presence. Welch explores evidence for republican amphitheaters that show signs of design by military engineers and argues that the elliptical plan of amphitheaters evolved from the wooden amphitheater erected in the Forum Romanum. From there, she examines the development of amphitheaters into the empire through the Colosseum, claiming that the lost Amphitheater of Statilius Taurus is the "missing link" in the evolution of Roman amphitheaters and that it must have had a façade in the Tuscan order; the Colosseum set a new precedent for the design of amphitheater building with its hierarchy of orders on the façade. This book includes an important chapter on how amphitheaters were received in the culturally Greek areas of the eastern half of the Roman Empire. While this book is the first to present so much interpretative information on amphitheaters in the republican period, some of Welch's conclusions are debated, and she may press too far the case with the Amphitheater of Statilius Taurus and her interpretation of the symbolism in the façade of the Colosseum. It is, nonetheless, a rewarding read that presents serious evidence and that poses provocative questions with important implications for our understanding of amphitheaters. In my undergraduate seminars on "Greek and Roman Sport and Spectacle," I always require my students to read it cover-to-cover, and we also discuss it after reading an important review that questions some of the evidence and conclusions: Frank Sear, "The Development of Roman Amphitheatres Down to the Colosseum, with Thoughts on That of Statilius Taurus and the Domus Aurea," *Journal of Roman Archaeology* 23 (2010) 505–509.

It will come as no surprise that the chief entertainments in Roman amphitheaters, gladiators, also have an extensive bibliography. Books on gladiators usually treat associated spectacles, namely the animal hunts and executions. Translated from the original French edition in 1970 (*Cruauté et civilization*), Roland Auguet's *Cruelty and Civilization: The Roman Games* (London: Allen & Unwin, 1972) has been made available in many different English reprints over the years by various presses. This was one of the first truly scholarly studies of Roman blood sports that attempted to examine Roman games objectively and in a Roman cultural context, rather than moralizing them. It is, however, rather outdated, and more current studies of the games are available. Georges Ville, *La gladiature en Occident des origins à la mort de Domitien* (Paris: École française de Rome, 1981), was a seminal and dense work on amphitheater games that is still a standard reference used by scholars, although it unfortunately has not been translated to English. Keith Hopkins, in his chapter "Murderous Games," in *Death and Renewal* (Cambridge: Cambridge University Press, 1983), argues that blood sports were an outgrowth of a militarized Roman society; that they served as a proxy for warfare during the period of peace ushered in by Augustus; and thus that they gained popularity during the Roman Empire, which also made amphitheaters a venue for political interaction and expression after the end of the Republic and the loss of the vote. It is an influential and important work, although the thesis may be overstated. Thanks in part to Welch's work, we also know now that amphitheater games were equally popular in the period of the Republic, before the imperial period and the loss of the vote.

Hopkins's chapter prompted exploration of subject-ruler interactions, as in Thomas Wiedemann's *Emperors and Gladiators* (London: Routledge, 1992). Importantly, Wiedemann discussed the amphitheater as a place that symbolized Roman imperial order and identity, as well as subject-ruler interactions. Paul Plass, *The Game of Death in Ancient Rome: Arena Sport and Political Suicide* (Madison: University of Wisconsin Press, 1995), discusses the politics of Roman games, their extravagance, and attempts to explain the sociological significance of violent spectacles. Alison Futrell's *Blood in the Arena: The Spectacle of Roman Power* (Austin: University of Texas Press, 1997) takes the idea of the amphitheater as a symbol of Roman identity and order and fleshes out the religious function of amphitheaters, especially their connections with emperor worship. She does not discuss the Colosseum much but concentrates rather on provincial amphitheaters and their associated games. She views Roman blood sport as a sort of human sacrifice to deified emperors, echoing the old practice of games for deceased noblemen, although many specialists find that her arguments in this regard go too far. It is, nevertheless, a valuable contribution to the study of Roman games and amphitheaters, as it is one of the few works in English to explore the religious aspects of amphitheaters.

Donald G. Kyle, *Spectacles of Death in Ancient Rome* (London: Routledge, 1998), deals with the disposal of dead gladiators and animals in amphitheaters and the lives of gladiators. Fik Meijer's *The Gladiators: History's Most Deadly*

Sport (London: Souvenir Press, 2003) is aimed at a general audience, affordable, and broadly covers gladiators, their lives and status, as well as *naumachiae*, executions, and animal spectacles. Although accessible, I find its coverage of many topics insufficient and sometimes inaccurate. A much better and engaging treatment of the same subjects, which are well-researched and presented with detailed notes, is Roger Dunkle's *Gladiators: Violence and Spectacle in Ancient Rome* (Harlow, UK: Pearson, 2008). Eckart Köhne and Cornelia Ewigleben (eds.), *Gladiators and Caesars* (Berkeley: University of California Press, 2000), is a much shorter text with essays on different components of amphitheaters games. Although not as exhaustive or as inclusive as Dunkle's book, it contains excellent color illustrations.

There are some other important works that tackle topics other than gladiatorial combats and *venationes*. Garrett G. Fagan, *The Lure of the Arena: Social Psychology and the Crowds at the Roman Games* (Cambridge: Cambridge University Press, 2011), interrogates how spectators responded to the games and the social psychology of the collective viewing of violent spectacles. He adeptly deploys modern sociological and psychological studies in his discussion of Roman practice. The association of the Colosseum with emperor worship, as well as the procession and appearance of divine images and attributes there, is the subject of my "The Procession and Placement of Imperial Cult Images in the Colosseum," *Papers of the British School at Rome* 82 (2014) 73–107. Amphitheater processions are treated more broadly in Jacob A. Latham, *Performance, Memory, and Processions in Ancient Rome: The Pompa Circensis from the Late Republic to Late Antiquity* (Cambridge: Cambridge University Press, 2016) 161–180, with little attention to the Colosseum. On Roman executions in Roman amphitheaters and, especially, in the Colosseum, the authoritative work is Kathleen M. Coleman, "Fatal Charades: Roman Executions Staged as Mythological Enactments," *Journal of Roman Studies* 80 (1990) 44–73. In fact, Coleman is a chief authority on Roman games, and her research is always exceptional and informative. Her article on the flooding of the Colosseum and *naumachiae* is another standard work: "Launching into History: Aquatic Displays in the Early Empire," *Journal of Roman Studies* 83 (1993) 48–74.

Martial's *Book of Spectacles*, written in praise of the emperor, is an important eyewitness account of some of the earliest Flavian games in the Colosseum, potentially the inaugural games; Coleman's translation and commentary, *Martial: Liber Spectaculorum* (Oxford: Oxford University Press, 2006), is detailed, thorough, and authoritative. It connects the text with the history, politics, and physical setting of Flavian Rome, while also commenting on Martial's intertextuality, the transmission of the text, and its interpretation. There is a wealth of historical, political, and literary background information in the front matter of her book, before the commentary even begins.

On the more generic subject of Greek and Roman sport and spectacle, there is no dearth of literature. Various textbooks and introductions include Nigel B. Crowther, *Sport in Ancient Times* (Westport, CT: Praeger, 2007); David Potter, *The Victor's Crown: A History of Ancient Sport from Homer to Byzantium* (Oxford: Oxford University Press, 2012); Thomas F. Scanlon (ed.), *Sport in the Greek and Roman Worlds*, 2 vols. (Oxford: Oxford University Press, 2014); Paul Christesen and Donald G. Kyle (eds.), *A Companion to Sport and Spectacle in Greek and Roman Antiquity* (Malden, MA: Wiley-Blackwell, 2014); and Donald G. Kyle, *Sport and Spectacle in the Ancient World*, 2nd ed. (Malden, MA: Wiley-Blackwell, 2015). Another book in the Witness to Ancient History series, Jerry Toner's *The Day Commodus Killed a Rhino: Understanding the Roman Games* (Baltimore: Johns Hopkins University Press, 2014), examines the significance of the Roman games in a Roman cultural context; it is a highly informative and engaging read that could be easily assigned to an undergraduate seminar. A great supplement to any course on the Roman games is Alison Futrell, *The Roman Games: A Sourcebook* (Malden, MA: Blackwell, 2006), which discusses Roman games and spectacle with reference to selected ancient sources. Anne Mahoney, *Roman Sports and Spectacles: A Sourcebook* (Newburyport, MA: Focus Publishing/R. Pullins Company, 2001), uses more inscriptions without sacrificing literary sources.

INDEX